I Am Matthew

Photo courtesy of Cynthia Cooper, The Tower Tribe: A Rat's Eye View.

I Am Matthew

A glimpse at homelessness like you've never seen before

Matthew Davidson

With Bethany Krafels

To those who didn't give up on me.

Table of Contents

Foreword

The journey that I have taken has been a perilous one, but the mistakes that I have made and the failures that have besieged my existence haven't been for naught. They say the price of wisdom is pain and the truths that I have found are paid in full. They are mine. Bought. Owned. Squandered. Found again.

My story is one of contradiction and contrast. Everything that was vile and filthy, deep within it held a glimmer of beauty. And everything of beauty, in the same manner, had an element of ugliness lurking inside. I gave up trying to understand everything that happened. A lot of it defies logic or reason, but such is the way of things and I have finally come to accept it.

My truths are just that, *my* truths. *My* perspectives. Life in the way that *I* saw it. It is not my objective to change the truths of others. Nor is it my goal to offer any solutions. My only wish is to share my experiences and, in doing so, offer a message of hope. All is not what it seems. It never is. The odds can be incredibly stacked against us, but in the end, the only thing that hinders our potential is our own fears, doubts and self-imposed limitations.

My tale is one of tragedy, of darkest despair. It is also a tale of triumph, a testament to the human spirit. I shouldn't be here today. I was a criminal, a drug addict and an alcoholic, homeless and cast aside for years. I was a savage of the lowest form. Economic conditions most definitely played a role in my becoming homeless, but ultimately it was my choices that brought me there, and it was my choices that brought me out. Few come back from where I was, yet anyone can. I know this because I did.

I Am Matthew

Fox in the Henhouse

I arrived in Fresno with a carry-on, small suitcase and some counter checks for one of my lines of credit. Although I was stepping into a world in which I knew nothing, I hadn't many concerns. I had always survived in the past, no matter what my situation was. Besides, this was California, *The Golden State*. Where better to make a fresh start than in the land where all of your dreams come true?

The first couple of years I was quite successful. My union membership was transferred to the local hall and it wasn't long before I got my foot in the door and had a lucrative construction job. Although my failed marriage and subsequent loss of my children haunted me to my core, outwardly, these were pretty good years. I was working steady and advancing in my craft. Additionally, I was enjoying the company of a nurturing soul named Nashelle who tended to my needs at a time when I really needed it. We had embarked on this new adventure together and it felt nice to share it with someone.

My companion and I drove a sporty little car and our efficient pad was located in the trendy Tower District, otherwise known as the entertainment center of Fresno. Each morning, the first things I saw when I opened up my eyes were the beautiful palm trees swaying in the breeze outside my window. Coming from Alaska, this alone felt exotic and offered the promise of a good life.

In 2006, the Tower District was magnificent. It brimmed with life and buzzed with an energy and anticipation that was unrivaled. Located only a few blocks from the city's college, one would expect to find the typical row of uninspiring college bars. This wasn't the case, it was so much more. Young and old, people from nearly every walk of life meshed here in a bright tapestry of music, art and expression. The nightlife was one of exuberant excess, of freedom and unrestrained impulse. It was definitely *the* place to be.

A good friend of ours was a bartender on the strip. If we slid her a couple of bucks across the counter we could drink for free until closing. Of course the parties didn't end when the bars closed, they were just getting started. We hit these splendid affairs pretty hard. Local DJs would frequently set up their systems and drop live house mixes right on the spot, keeping us spinning until dawn. Night, after night, we attended these events which brought us into the ranks of "cool folk". We met more and more people and were considered regular faces at anything that was "anything".

Throughout all of this, I was working full-time. I guess I figured that I could have my cake and eat it too. I loved to party, but I told myself that if it ever affected my job, I would stop. Strangely enough, as a result of this lifestyle, I became even better at my job. In fact, the more haggard I was, the harder I worked. I suppose that I was in denial of eventually having to put the brakes on this wild ride.

I kept it running for quite some time and, of course, it escalated daily. Before long, I had rekindled former relationships with cocaine, then finally meth, ecstasy, mushrooms and acid. There wasn't anything that I didn't have access to. Methamphetamine (crank, meth, ice, glass, whichever formula or recipe I took at the time) seemed to be a good fit for me. The high that it provided suited my personality and tendencies well and it easily became my drug of choice. Beyond the fact that I didn't need to eat or sleep while under its influence, it also seemed to make me impervious to pain and/or hardship. Above all, it gave me drive. I know this sounds crazy, but completing tasks (regardless of whether they were large or small) with such a maniacal fervor made me feel good.

Although it was a fast life, my inevitable descent was actually quite gradual. Throughout this affair, I achieved just enough success to lull myself into thinking that everything was in order. In hindsight, I realize that I was doomed from the start, I simply chose not to see it.

As time went on, I was an integral part of all of the different social circles. My magnetic personality has always been a draw for me and drugs only amplified it. At this point, I was drinking for free at nearly every bar in the neighborhood and eating for free at a lot of the cool restaurants. I knew all of the DJs, strippers, dealers and anyone who mattered in the party circuit. I was *in*.

I'm not quite sure exactly how long this pattern continued, but eventually a series of events caused a fracture in this parade of parties. It began when several police officers were shot by gang members and the resultant high speed chase careened through the Tower

District. This changed a lot of things. Battle lines were drawn and everyone in the area suffered because of it.

The police aggressively stepped up their presence, as did the gang involved, the Bulldogs. This led to a lot of friction and hardship for everyone. In addition, the unemployment rate for Fresno County had crept up to almost forty percent. On top of that, nearly one in three people were using meth. The entire city was steeped in an air of hopelessness, frustration and unease. It was a recipe for disaster.

The chain of events that ultimately led me to becoming homeless seemed to move excruciatingly slow. You would think that anyone with a sound mind would have been able to foresee the impending consequence, but I didn't. Again, maybe I just didn't care to see it. The fact of the matter is, it happened because I failed to plan ahead. The construction trade has always had employment gaps. As the economy worsened, the jobs became less frequent and increasingly farther away from Fresno. I eventually started to fall behind on our bills.

The car was the first to go. We drove it for quite a while without insurance, and even longer without making any payments, but it was finally repossessed. I think we owed less than a thousand dollars on it, but we just couldn't cover it. We managed to hang on to our apartment for ten or eleven months longer.

Initially, the guys from my job outfit picked me up for work, but with the jobs getting further and further apart, the company finally let me go. I can't help but think that the outfit was just sick and tired of leaving forty-five minutes early for work to pick me up. Not that I blamed them. It wasn't more than ninety days later that we lost the apartment. The landlord gave us a lot of breaks but we just couldn't get enough scraped together to keep it.

I've always been bad at saving money. Obviously I should have buckled down and set some cash aside, however, my lifestyle wouldn't allow for that. Every moment that I wasn't at work consisted of pursuing my poisons. Our last days spent at our apartment were in the garage. The landlord let us pile all of our stuff inside after vacating the apartment. He gave us an additional week to find a new place but we were unable to find one. Now, after having first lost our mode of transportation and then our apartment, we lost all of our belongings. It was just as well, I suppose, for we had nowhere to take them.

We bounced around for quite a while after that, couch-surfing, sleeping in garages, etc.... We weren't grounded anywhere for more than a couple of days at a time. An opportunity finally surfaced for us to stay at a drug house located on the far edge of the neighborhood. The owner had been dreaming of diversifying a bit to increase his revenue, so he added a few girls to the mix to provide additional services. It was a three bedroom house; two of the rooms were used for the girls to work in, as well as sleep in, and the master bedroom remained the area for other business.

The house was in decent condition but the large, fenced-in yard was in disarray and the garage was in shambles. I made an agreement with the owner to first remedy these initial construction problems before switching gears to security detail in exchange for being able to stay in the garage. My companion originally joined me but didn't stay long (the environment wasn't as favorable for her as it was for me). With her gone, I worked hard and partied even harder.

Once the yard and garage were in order, I focused my efforts on the house's operations. I made sure that the doors stayed locked, things ran orderly and the girls, the homeowner and his wares stayed safe. As guests arrived, I locked up behind them and offered coffee, tea or water. I was polite and engaged them in conversation to put them at ease. I saw to their comfort and made sure that everyone not only stayed safe, but also felt safe.

This arrangement went on for quite a while and it appeared that everyone was content. I had a comfortable place to stay. The guests were treated well and were happy with their services. The girls were being productive, felt safe and loved how much I doted on them. The owner appreciated that his revenue was up and was happy that he could look ahead and plan other potential earning opportunities. The business environment was clean, safe and respectful. As you can imagine, this is not the usual nature of such places. Not surprisingly, it didn't last long.

One evening, I felt very on edge. Everyone in the house kept trying to put me at ease, but I could sense something was wrong. I was suspicious that one of the new guests, who we had recently entertained, meant me harm. Throughout the night, the doors were repeatedly left unlocked and the lights continually turned off. Over and over, I would resecure the entry points and adjust the lighting.

As the night wore on, one of the girls kept asking for help with her laptop. Her workstation was set up so that our backs were to both doors. A lamp had been placed on the table, shining brightly. Unbeknownst to them, I could see their plot unfolding from a mile away. Every time I looked up, all of the other lights were off, leaving me in a blinding circle of light that I couldn't see out of. This series of events dragged on until dawn.

A single mother had been staying at the house with her two kids. She had already cooked them breakfast and the kids were getting ready for school. Suddenly, as if on cue, she brought her children into the back bedroom. I heard the door lock behind them. The girl that I had been helping "conveniently" had to use the bathroom. I heard the door lock behind her as well. I knew what time it was. As I got up from the table the new guest suddenly appeared. "Come to the back yard," he barked, "I want to talk to you." I turned and walked towards the back door with the stranger in tow.

As I slowly opened the door and stepped outside, I took a large, quick step and whirled around to face him. Just as I expected, his fist whistled past where my head had just been. Instantly, he had a razor sharp 8-inch hunting knife in his hand. He started advancing toward me, slowly working the knife back and forth in front of him. I stepped back in diagonal angles. First away from his knife, and then towards it, being careful not to settle into a pattern.

The morning sun was at my back, it was just starting to burn the dew off of the grass. He didn't know that I was ready for him. I was always ready. Underneath the sleeves of my jersey I had a pair of woven Kevlar arm guards that I had acquired from the glass factory in Selma. Already in my hand, but hidden, was my dagger. I didn't let him see either. He kept backing me across the yard, so sure of himself, that he fell into a rhythm. This tends to be a common mistake.

By now, the warm sun was gently caressing the nape of my neck. With amazing clarity, I could hear the birds chirping and the insects whizzing by. I could hear the kids inside the house, still getting ready for school. All of my senses were sharpened and acute. With only four feet left until he had me cornered into the back of the fence, I decided on this beautiful spring morning that I would have to kill him. It almost wasn't fair. I still hadn't shown my weapon and in his overconfidence he thought I was unarmed.

I was moments away from making my move when he quickly threw down his knife and took a step back. I casually traipsed past him and exited the yard. In the driveway, I narrowly missed his two cohorts who had just come around the side of the house to assist him. "Everybody around here seems just a touch too slow," I muttered over my shoulder as I walked away. My intentions had apparently become very clear to him by the look in my eyes. Fortunately for both of us, he realized his folly.

Of course that wasn't the only incident that occurred at this particular house. Neither the drug nor prostitution industry are known for their cut of the moral cloth, so to speak. There were frequent situations to contend with. The most dangerous and life-altering event occurred while the homeowner was away on a short business trip.

There I was, the fox in the henhouse. The coop was empty except for myself and the three working girls. Business had been shut down for the night and we were all looking forward to some much needed recreation. My only orders were to keep the girls safe and to not let any other clients inside. That sounded easy enough. A short time later, the girls called over some of their girlfriends and together we spent the evening taking big bong rips of meth. It was initially shaping up to be a great night.

When the doorbell rang, I got up and looked through the peephole. Standing outside was a Bulldog dropout who had been making a lot of trouble in the area. He was highest on the list of people **not** allowed in. Thieving, robbing and raping were his calling cards. However, in the perverse way of how things go down on the streets, the homeowner still did business with him. When the head girl told me to let him in, I was hesitant. I knew that trouble would come in the door with him, but I had been instructed to defer to her word. The homeowner was sweet on her so, of course, she was the one who was really in charge.

It wasn't long before he became aggressive. The more I tried to placate and calm him, the worse it got. "It doesn't get any better than this," I explained, "be cool man. We've got a fat bag and a bunch of girls. Let's just have fun." I soon realized that he was under the influence of KJ, otherwise known as PCP or Angel Dust. KJ is known to give its user temporary insanity, incredible strength and extremely violent tendencies. I knew that we were in trouble.

As the night progressed, things continued to escalate. Finally, the owner of the house came back with several validated and well-established gang members in tow. They stepped into the back office and closed the door behind them, signifying that they weren't to be interrupted. Not five minutes had passed when the Dropout, now in a froth, pushed his way into the room. Everyone at the table paused and looked at the door, dumbfounded at his vociferous lack of respect. He closed the door behind him which blocked me, security, away from my principle.

I forced my way in and ordered him to leave. He furiously wheeled around and started berating me in front of the men gathered at the table. Enraged, he screamed, "I'M TAKING OVER THIS PLACE." I looked the owner in the eye and asked "You got cleanup?" He was the type of guy who liked to appear that he was in control of every situation. With a smug look on his face, he informed me that he would indeed handle cleanup.

As the men remained seated, the Dropout became increasingly unstable. He relentlessly taunted me and refused to calm down. Seeing the situation develop, and realizing that it had become untenable, I knew that I needed to take immediate action. My eyes darted about my adjacent area until they came to rest upon an old claw hammer lying on a dresser with some tools. I discreetly took it in my hand and hid it behind my leg.

I was scared. Scared that I would kill him. Scared that I wouldn't kill him. Scared that he would kill me. There were a lot of thoughts whirling around in my head. I knew that his extreme condition would require extreme actions, so before I could shirk away from the horrid task that lay before me, I struck. It split his head wide open at the crown, just over his left ear. His skull glistened slickly, only for an instant, before the rushing waves of bright blood swept away the sight.

Screaming, and with his arms still over his head, he leapt up and started sprinting about the house. Blood sprayed onto the ceiling and splattered the walls in a grisly pattern. I followed him, striking again and again. Most of the poundings rained down on his elbows and forearms. Every little bit, I would switch directions and head him off, meeting him with a stiff arm and a sharp, well-aimed blow.

It didn't take long for these impacts to take their toll. In a matter of seconds, which felt as if they had stretched on for hours, I had him cornered. In front of me, his lifeless body slid down the living room wall and slumped to the floor. I looked around and was amazed at how much blood there was. It was everywhere. I could feel it squishing under my feet in the carpet. As he started twitching, I turned, stuck the hammer in my pants and walked out. Like previously arranged, cleanup was left for the homeowner to handle. Still seated motionless around the table, but in clear view of the events which unfolded in the next room, their dumbfounded expressions followed me out the door.

I spent the next three days hiding out with a stripper that I knew across town. I was very concerned that brain swelling would end his life. Fortunately, he survived. Unfortunately, this meant that I had created a life-long enemy. His brothers, who were active gang members, were on the hunt to fill me up with holes so I had to lay low for quite a while. Additionally, I had no idea if the cops were involved so I avoided the area for that reason as well.

I feel very fortunate that neither of us lost our life that day. Things could have easily gone very differently in either direction. I still sicken at the memory of that beating, and it definitely disturbed me to know that I was capable of such things. I thank God that I did not kill him; I'm not sure that I could have ever emotionally recovered if I had. This last incident, without question, was one of the most pivotal moments of my entire life. It marked the beginning of a downward spiral which ultimately led to years of agony and pain.

All said, I spent three long years living on the streets in Fresno, California. When I say "on the streets" I literally mean just that. No shelters. No aid of any kind. Nothing. You must be wondering how I managed to survive that long without any type of assistance. Go ahead, you do the math. Suffice to say, me being homeless didn't mean that I was weak or stupid. At the time, I had no real respect for consequence. This was certainly an asset in my fight for survival, but it was also a detriment to my humanity. I knew that in order to preserve it, I would have to follow a few self-imposed rules.

The rules which I vowed to keep were as follows:

1) I would never steal from or take advantage of good, hard-working people.
2) I would never hurt anybody that wasn't trying to hurt me.

3) I would always help somebody who needed help.
4) I would never deny anyone food, water or clothing if it were available to me.
5) I would always follow basic "man code", like keeping my word, showing respect, etc....

On occasion there were situations where I was forced to compromise my principles and I was unable to abide by my own set of rules. This bothered me tremendously. For the most part, I went to great lengths to preserve this integrity within myself. It was so necessary. Out there, with your pride and self-respect already shaved down to a sliver, it's crucial to keep this code, this core dignity. When you have nothing else in the world, you still have that. If you don't, it's unlikely that you will ever make it out alive.

The Trap

I'm not going to lie, in the beginning it almost felt like a game being homeless. I was faster, stronger, quicker and smarter than those around me. I knew things about things. Raised in rural Alaska, I spent most of my youth honing my survival skills. Field craft, hunting, fishing, shooting, tracking, Native American lore and techniques were all explored and developed. As a scout in the Army, these skills were perfected even further.

Later in life, I trained in MMA and fought in a few professional fights. I had always been fascinated with all types of martial arts, not just the execution of skills, but also the mindset and tactics behind them. All of these proficiencies served me quite well in this "game" of survival. Working in the construction trade for many years also came in handy. When you can see at a glance how things are built, well, let's just say that locks on doors are pretty much meaningless.

Re-united once again with Nashelle, we were back to couchsurfing with friends of ours. Of course these arrangements never lasted long so we were continually working towards securing our next location. I used my tactical and security abilities, as well as my carpentry skills, to barter for lodging. As time went on, I noticed a recurring theme. As soon as I had altered whatever situation that I had been brought on to remedy, my worth was no longer recognized, appreciated or even wanted. In fact, I was often perceived as a threat by the very people who I had initially helped.

I guess in todays "something for nothing" mindset, that's just how it goes down. Once my work was finished, situations were repeatedly fabricated to justify our departure. One can imagine how unstable these situations became considering that everybody in "the game" had ulterior motives. Compounding this was the fact that women are considered either property or a financial asset out on the street. My companion was targeted without fail. This greatly changed the dynamic of many of our living situations.

The last place we lived under such an arrangement, we referred to as The Trap. It was a large, turn of the century house on a corner lot, situated deep in the heart of Bulldog territory. Those of us on the streets referred to this particular neighborhood that we lived in, and hustled in, as The Zone. It was derived from the term "war zone". That it was.

Shootings, stabbings and beatings were a daily happening in this area and police presence was smothering. They aggressively patrolled the area and frequently made raids with SWAT and the armored carrier that we liked to call "the tank". Their helicopter was constantly circling the neighborhood and lighting up areas with its bazillion candlepower spotlight. We often made sport of it by shining cheap laser lights into the cockpit at night. We had been told that green lasers would blind their night vision, so of course, we made

14

every effort to do so. We all hated that thing. I knew every cut and could outrun any foot or vehicle pursuit in the hood, but the chopper was a tough nut to crack. It was the bane of our existence.

The streets outside this particular house were a virtual open-air market for prostitution and drugs. Everybody in the city knew that this is where you went to satisfy your vices. The owners of the house lived out of town and an elder from the neighborhood stayed there to "maintain" the property. Here's what was really going on....

The Bulldogs had taken over the place and were using it for their business operations. Whores and drugs were bought, sold and used there. Stolen vehicles were taken there to be hidden, stripped and then sold for parts. Fugitives would slide in and either change their clothes to alter their appearance or rest until darkness would mask their movements. Stolen goods were stockpiled there until they could be brokered. Its central location made it perfect for all of these operations.

During this timeframe, Fresno was owned by the Bulldogs. Period. There were approximately 4500 validated members, however, the numbers were even greater when you factored in the up-and-coming youths and sympathizers. Some estimates showed an active membership closer to 12,000. Most all of the poor neighborhoods had some sort of fealty, or allegiance, to them. No other gangs were allowed to reside in or operate within the city. This was enforced with an iron fist.

Initially, the Bulldogs were predominantly Hispanic, but as time went on the ranks began swelling with members of all races. There was an uneasy truce with a white gang, known as the Fresnecks, but nothing official. Because they were so loosely organized, a truce or "ghetto pass" was hard to sustain with anyone.

As it was in my case, it was pretty much earned on a day-to-day basis.

Originating from a larger, more established and more powerful organization, the Bulldogs claimed their independence sometime in the 80s with a bloody revolt. Tired of being spent as front line troops and being taxed heavily by the hierarchy, they claimed their "freedom" and became bitter rivals with just about every other faction since. They were so violent and so fiercely independent that much of their time was spent warring, even amongst themselves. Despite the fact that they were very loosely organized, they were almost reminiscent of feudal warlords.

It was very hard to keep everything straight for an outsider such as myself, not to mention very, very dangerous. I had no business being there and I am fortunate to have survived. Life was held cheaply in those parts; no thought at all was given to claiming another's life. Operating independently and not showing allegiance to any one organization, while at the same time showing proper respect and deference, was an intricate balance that was very hard for me to maintain. Of course, for my livelihood I had to assert relevance in certain areas of commerce, yet I couldn't make too many waves or it was certain death.

I was unaware of these gang-related details when I agreed to fix up the garage at The Trap in exchange for being allowed to stay in it. The state of things quickly became clear upon my arrival, but for the moment, I wasn't too concerned. They seemed to keep to the main house, preferring it to the dingy, old garage. It was in a horrible state of neglect and disrepair with trash, filth and excrement piled high.

My first day or so was spent mucking the place out and discarding all of the refuse. Although hard work, those were heady times. I could see the potential in the place and it felt good to finally be proactive about my situation. I was able to be creative and use my acquired skills to improve the quality of life for myself and my companion. After a few labor-intensive days, I had the place emptied out and cleaned. I had found some disinfectant and scrubbed it deep into the pores of the concrete, thus abolishing the smell which permeated it.

The next couple of weeks I spent furnishing it. I traveled up and down the alleys for miles on end to find furniture, rugs and other goods to dress the place up. I even spent an entire day dragging back a couch and loveseat set. It was grueling work but well worth the effort. For our bed, I made a large hammock out of a ten-foot section of chain-link fencing. I ran pipes through the links of the fencing and then suspended it with additional chains attached to the pipes. Once stable, I topped it with a futon mattress which I had also found on my travels. Finally, we were sleeping in style.

The once soiled garage had been completely transformed into a home. *Our* home. In addition to our sleeping quarters, it also contained a small kitchen, a living room and a clothing/storage area. Carpeting stretched wall-to-wall and several eucalyptus branches were arranged in vases throughout the room. These not only looked nice, but helped mask the smell of the honey bucket behind the screen in the corner which served as our bathroom area.

Our new home was small, yet very comfortable. It felt great to have a safe place to sleep as well as having the ability to lock up our stuff when we left. We watched movies and listened to music on my recently acquired laptop. We even swung from the hammock when the mood struck. Life was really good for a bit, almost normal. But true to form, just when things began to show a glimmer of promise on the streets, they quickly fell apart.

About that time, I had started working for cash with a neighborhood tree trimmer. Up until that point, cash had been in very short supply. The job felt promising and I was confident that I would be able to advance our situation in short order. Constantly moving around, combined with the daily uncertainty, really began to wear on me. I was yearning for a place to call my own and I believed that things were finally on the right track.

Unfortunately, while I was at work, more and more attention was being paid to the garage. Now that it was fixed up, the Bulldogs wanted it for themselves. Also of interest to them was my companion who was at home alone. She was very attractive and fiercely loyal to me. It seemed this made her an irresistible target. I came home one day and found her incoherent. I later found out that some of the girls from the house had fixed her lunch, drugged her and then stole my laptop. I was incensed, but conveniently, nobody knew anything.

When I arrived home the following day, I noticed that she had barricaded herself inside the garage. As soon as I walked up, the Bulldogs who had gathered around the door quickly scattered and went back into the house. She was crying and very distraught so it took a bit of time to coax out of her what had happened. Apparently one of the Bulldogs had told her, "You're mine now, as is the garage, and we will do with you as we wish."

Without a second thought, I immediately turned and walked up to the house. Kicking in the door, I leaped through a handful of Bulldogs and punched the culprit in the face. As he flew across the room, I turned and walked back out to the yard. My shirt was pulled off in a haste to show them I was unarmed. I stood there on that lawn, in the hot Fresno sun, and waited for the entire crew of Bulldogs to come out and face me in a one-sided fight which had an outcome I already knew. I waited for them to come out and kill me.

Standing there in that yard was a turning point of sorts. In my aimless life, one that had become without purpose or depth, it felt good to finally stand for something. I needed to draw that line in the sand. I needed to stand as a man. To break that chain of compromise and concession was important, and although it did not free me, it changed me. I wasn't willing to die because nothing mattered. I was willing to die because it did. It had been forever since I felt anything like that, and it wasn't until I was faced with an impending death, that I realized how much I truly wanted to live.

There was a lot of yelling and threats hurled at me, but nobody ever came out. I waited for a while before returning to the garage. There, I grabbed my machete and told Nashelle to pack a travel kit. As darkness fell, more and more Bulldogs began to arrive. We could hear them screaming at us, "You'll never leave the hood alive." That's when we left.

The Bulldogs were certain that they had run us out and quickly forgot about us. What they didn't know is that we had holed up on the second floor of an abando, or abandoned site, less than a block away. These old apartments had a clear line of sight to The Trap. There I watched, waited and made a half-dozen Molotov cocktails. I siphoned gas from cars and used old 40 bottles that were littered about the alley. I melted Styrofoam into the gas to make it more viscous and mixed in laundry detergent to provide phosphorus.

My intention was to learn their patterns and to catch them sleeping, then to destroy them in a devastating fire-bomb assault. They had backed me into a corner and threatened me and mine. What they hadn't counted on was that their idle threats had unleashed a beast within me. I watched them for three days and three nights. I knew exactly when I was going to hit. There was a pack of them outside stripping some stolen cars. All I had to do was wait for them to pass out, for they had been drinking all day in the hot sun while they worked. As soon as darkness fell, and they were all passed out, I would strike.

As I watched and waited for the exact moment to attack, a flurry of squad cars and unmarked vehicles swarmed the location. I was forced to stand down and wait for the area to cool off. There wasn't a chance of following through with my plans at that point.

Ironically, being arrested for grand theft auto saved those gangster's lives; more than likely it saved mine as well. It still shames me that on that day I was going to kill a half-dozen of my associates. By thinking three or four moves ahead at all times, I should have been able to avoid situations like these. Going forward, I knew that I had to become even more vigilant when it came to our safety.

A Siren's Song

We were constantly on the move. Things would turn hostile and dangerous at the drop of a hat and situations were routinely manufactured to meet the perverse whims of those who operated in our area. Because of this, nowhere was ever safe so staying mobile was usually the best policy. It was a delicate balance though. Once you stopped moving you could become a victim. But fluidity, although a powerful tool, also had its drawbacks. You could never amass any amount of comfort items or negotiable goods, at least not if you wanted to move swiftly. And anyone on the streets knows that if you're moving slowly, you might as well not be moving at all.

The truth of it is, you just get plain tired. You can never really sleep because that's when you get hurt, or your stuff gets taken or your girl gets attacked. The only rest you get is when you're so exhausted that you simply don't care anymore what happens to you. When you're static, you're nothing but a target, but sometimes you just have to recon the block, weigh the odds and hunker down. To be able to sit down and eat, to take a sponge bath, to check and re-pack your provisions or maybe even to have the pleasure of some physical intimacy with your lover is often a siren's song that's impossible to resist.

The most alluring of all, and hardest to traverse, was getting some rest. When you're constantly on the move, sleep deprivation, psychological stress, starvation and dehydration all take their toll. There would be times when not only my body would refuse to press on, but my mind as well. Unfortunately, while in this state, poor choices were often made. Deliriously exhausted, I have stumbled into vacant houses and collapsed onto the floor, only to be startled awake by the homeowner or realtor coming into the room yelling. With both of us stunned, the potential for somebody to get hurt was high. I've had to jump up and sprint away from a dead sleep, leaving behind whatever was not immediately on my person. I have awakened to discover my backpack and bike gone more times than I can count.

The conundrum is, as much as I yearned for a nice, long, comfortable rest, I hated having to do it. Unless great care was taken, it always ended badly. You can never let your guard down out there, not even for an instant. Sleep became the enemy. I would push on and on, much longer than I ever should have, denying myself such a luxury. That's not to say it didn't happen. I've crashed out in dumpster enclosures, park benches, storefronts, clumps of bushes, etc... only to be awoke by somebody either trying to steal my stuff or thinking that I was a corpse. Whenever I did find a good, safe place to rest I would often "bank" sleep hours. Sometimes I would sleep for three days, giving my body a much needed chance to heal and repair.

While on the move, our survival depended on utilizing abandos, or vacant houses. Fortunately for us, the horrible economy facilitated quite a few of them. There were entire neighborhoods that were empty. With the staggering unemployment rate, it was hard for most to keep their homes. Banks would foreclose on houses, one after another. The occupants would be evicted and the homes would sit with a sign in the yard touting its attributes. Cleaned, emptied and ready, silently waiting for a buyer that would probably not come for quite some time.

For the most part, there was never less than one empty house per block, and the blocks stretched on and on throughout the city. These vacant houses were quite a benefit to us as their uses were many. We would treat them as weigh stations when moving across the city. A drink of water could be offered from the spigot at one place, somewhere to cook something at another. Sometimes they were just a place to duck in and safely nap away the brutal afternoon heat.

It was relatively easy to get inside of these abandos. Having a keen eye and a background in construction made just about anything accessible. Second story dwellings were the easiest to enter as it was almost a guarantee that a window would be left unlocked on the second floor. Single story dwellings would sometimes be accessed through the gable vent or basement windows. Any building with a roof mount, AC unit or swamp cooler already had a 16 x 16 cut opening which offered easy access as well. Attached garages were frequently a home's weak link and even the highest quality doorknob was no match for someone in possession of a pipe wrench. The fact of the matter was, if one was difficult to access, I would simply head next door. The numbers certainly played in my favor in that wasteland of economic blight.

There were a few of us who viewed these abandos as a renewable resource, so to speak. When used, great care was taken to not be seen. The place was cleaned up and all traces of our presence was hidden. This preserved its availability and helped ensure that it was there for the next time that it was needed. I always did as little damage as possible for three main reasons. First, I didn't want to betray my presence. Second, I wanted to keep my charges to a minimum if I were ever to be discovered. Last but not least, I did so out of respect to the property owner.

I had no desire to possess these places or to profit off of them, nor did I want to loot them or destroy them as others did. I just wanted to be safe. To relax and rest a bit. To prepare a meal or bathe. These basic human needs seem so trivial to average citizens, but they are a sought after luxury for those living out on the streets.

Sometimes I would lay there, and just for a moment, let my thoughts explore what it would be like to live there. What my routines would be. Where I would place the coffee maker. Which room I would sleep in. Where I would tether the dogs. I didn't allow myself these drifts into fantasy for very long or very often. It only made the ache so much worse knowing that I could no longer have any of this, knowing that I was only pretending, for just a moment, that I was a real person living a normal life.

Others were not as savvy or respectful with regards to the abandos. They would "blow it out", as we called it. Not only were they careless about not being seen or heard, but a lot of times they were downright destructive. More than just leaving a mess, quite often they would gut the place for recyclables. I found this to be bad for a variety of reasons. Most importantly, if other residents knew of our presence their behavior certainly became more aggressive towards us.

Neighbors would frequently call the police. Homeowners checking on their property would come absolutely unglued if they discovered you. Same went for the realtors. All of which were quick to dial the authorities. A lot of times this would lead to an area becoming unusable. The very nature of my existence mandated that I be as discreet as possible. On the streets there are always people trying to hurt you or get at what's yours. The less waves you made in your daily life, the more you were able to deal with the "random" situations that arose.

I always felt that public opinion was important. I'm quite certain that most of the time I "looked the part" to your average citizen: a homeless drug addict and a criminal. However, I constantly attempted to be unobtrusive and to remain unnoticed. If observed or confronted, I continually tried to be courteous and respectful in order to put them at ease. Nobody has time for a daylight fight with a citizen and you certainly didn't want them to be placing a call to the authorities. These altercations would only rob you of precious energy, some of which you may have needed to save your life. Because of this, I felt that taking these extra steps to avoid detection and confrontation paid for themselves in full.

Other than their calls to report us, the residents pretty much left us alone. I think most of them knew that at the rate things were going it would only be a matter of time before they and their families were out on the streets as well. This was reflected in all areas of town but especially in the poorest sections. As a rule rather than the exception, these people were the most generous.

On one occasion, while scavenging with a Hmong girl in the roughest sections of her route, the residents actually came out and offered us food as we dug through their trash. Of course we graciously accepted their generous gift. We enjoyed the steaming hot, homemade burrito and ice cold Coca-Cola with a light heart and a twinkle in our eyes.

Simple acts of kindness made such an impact on those of us who had nothing and it really did seem that the people with the least to spare often gifted the most. Perhaps this was because they knew their position in society was only a single thread away from ours. As I write this, that girl is now dead. Yet another casualty of the streets.

If I weren't utilizing an abando, I was on the move. Simple as that. Like a hyena, I wandered the night. With my companion left behind to guard our belongings, I was able to focus specifically on the tasks at hand. Every detail was noticed, weighed and catalogued in my passing. Items of worth were immediately secured and cached, to be sold or bartered as soon as possible. As part of my nightly routine I would pass through at least a handful of my regular locations to scout for food, water, negotiable goods and/or a place to rest, but I also made it a habit to continually check for new potential opportunities while on my route as well.

I would never really "case" a place, I was just fully aware of any and all details at all times. Every angle, every pattern, every weakness, every strength, etc... was constantly being processed in my mind. Who needed what? How active were the police? What was the gang activity in that particular area? How would I acquire something? How would I transport it? All of these questions and more were constantly swirling around in my head. It seemed that I was always thinking of the next move, the next 5-way-trade, the next sack, the next sale, the next acquisition, the next conflict. It never ended.

Not having a phone, these transactions turned into long, drawn-out affairs that were laden with defeated expectations and wasted time. Apparently, no one else in the world held my time as important as I did. So much of it was blundered on trips back and forth to show items. A lot of it was spent in waiting. My focus would immediately shift if food were found sometime throughout this process. Every effort would then be committed to getting it carefully transferred back to wherever I was staying at the time. Plans were pretty much a complete waste of time. Even if I did have a course carefully plotted, some eventuality would upset it along the way. It was maddening at times and I was almost always in a frustrated state of mind.

Considering that I was rarely adequately fed or rested, I can't help but wonder how I didn't come apart. Maybe this swirling miasma of loosely organized thought kept me from thinking about how bad things really were. Maybe that's the only way I was able to keep my sanity in this mess that had become my life.

To live in such a way, without parameters or limits or restraints, definitely kept me alive. My instincts and reflexes had developed to a keen edge. My movements often defied logic and were unpredictable to those around me. This was a necessity out on the grimy streets that were fraught with danger and filled with predators that watch your every move. However, by living this way I lost a little bit of myself each and every day.

It eventually got to the point where survival was literally the only thing on my mind. Hope was long gone and dreams for a better life were of the distant past. Always moving. Always searching. Not even knowing what for, but just hoping that I'd find it and more importantly, that I'd know it when I did.

Perhaps I subconsciously did this so that I wouldn't have to face the disgust I felt towards myself. Here I was, a lawless drug addict and a father who had walked away from his precious daughters. I had initially convinced myself that I had done them a favor by leaving, yet I couldn't shake my guilt. Honestly, I knew the very moment the wheels on that plane lifted off the ground that I had made the wrong choice, I just felt that it was too late to turn back. That choice still haunts me.

Furthermore, I was no longer a highly trained professional at the top of my trade, but rather someone who had been reduced to stealing and foraging to sustain my existence. That's who I had become. A man who loved to see smiles and bring kind words to others, now someone who could only show menace and danger in order to survive. That's who I had become. I didn't like the new me, but I knew that in order to survive out on the streets, I had to accept who I had become.

Cash for Keys

Large houses, especially those in a good location, would inevitably draw other squatters. Sometimes this would work for a bit as security tasks could be rotated and food procurement shared. Almost without fail, however, increased numbers led to squabbles and brought extra attention which usually resulted in us having to leave. We were all fiercely territorial about a good spot. Our survival depended on it. Violence was the primary language out there and knives, machetes and axes were the tools often brought to bear.

Contrarily, if another squatter asked, and could bring something of benefit to the situation, they were rarely refused. There's strength in numbers, or so they say. This thought process led to numerous small tribal bands of homeless people who would often clash. I was usually able to maneuver myself to a clear tactical advantage quickly, which meant that I didn't have to exercise my proficiency in martial arts very often. The key to this was being ready to do so without hesitation and making this fact very well known to everyone around me.

On one occasion, I worked out an arrangement at an unoccupied fourplex located off Belmont Street. It was all by itself next to the canal and its discreet placement and location made it the perfect site to hole up in. Its windows and doors were covered with sheets of plywood and its forlorn, vacant presence was hardly noticed from the road.

The lady, who I had made the arrangement with, told us that the property owners had allowed her to stay in one of the apartments. We were allowed to stay there as well, in exchange for cleaning and fixing up the other units. The power and water were still on so it was only a short while before the area was scrubbed clean and we had all of the comforts of home.

Naturally, it was all too good to be true. As it turned out, the lady and her boyfriend were KJ addicts. They were always screaming and throwing things at each other and it was only a couple of days before we saw that he had pounded her face into a swollen mask of pain. Grotesquely lumped and bruised, she spit blood at him and snarled "You hit like a girl," before chasing him off with a knife. It was quiet for about a week. I came home one day with some cash in my pocket after finding a rare side job. I was excited to show my companion that I had done well.

Nearing our room, I heard shouting and noticed that our door had been kicked in. My pulse quickened. In a flash, I pulled out a pair of knives from my waistline and stepped inside. Once in the room, I discovered that four Mexicans had backed my companion into the hallway. They were unable to grab her, for she was swinging my machete at them with sharp strokes. Now, surrounded by gleaming steel, they immediately whipped out their cell phone and called the police. As they withdrew, I secured the door and made sure that Nashelle was unharmed.

It was all very surreal. First, coming home to this surprise, and second, that it culminated in the intruders calling the authorities. That just doesn't happen on the streets. The police were there within minutes and immediately asked who had the legal right to reside there. The others quickly replied, "We do." Without reviewing any kind of lease agreement or paperwork of any sort, the officers told us that we had ten minutes to gather our things before vacating the premises.

Hurriedly, I grabbed as many of our belongings as I could. After throwing them outside, I drug them across the alley where I piled them in a large heap. Knowing what was about to go down, I sent my companion into the Tower District to find a friend of mine who always had his pit bull by his side. Sure enough, as soon as the cops left, more and more of them began to congregate. They filtered in, one by one, until seven of them lined the top tier of the fourplex. Leaning over the rail, they silently watched me across the alley. I assumed they were waiting for dark. As efficiently as I could, and ever so watchful, I got all of our possessions ready for transport. I was just about packed up by the time Nashelle arrived back with my friend and his pit bull, Sadie.

Sadie girl, bless her heart, was just a doll to us. She knew what was up. From the very moment she saw the Mexicans all lined up, she bristled and snarled in their direction, as if she could sense their intentions. As soon as she arrived on the scene, most of the group left. Their leader remained and jabbered into his phone. We needed a bike trailer and some shopping carts to transport our possessions, so I left my friend and Sadie in charge while I rushed off to acquire them. I was gone about an hour and managed to get enough cartage to haul away all of our stuff. Apparently, as soon as I had left, the Mexicans started trickling back in, all decked out in heavy Ben Davis work pants, work coats, boots and heavy gloves.

Now that they were "dog proofed", their intentions were to make a move while I was away. That was not a good course of action for them. Sadie girl savaged one of them so horribly that most of them left immediately. When I returned, I openly laughed at the few who remained on the rail. I squatted down beside Sadie and pointed at them while I talked to her. Apparently, that was the last straw for them as they all broke away after that. We were finally able to load up and roll out without incident. And not a moment too soon, darkness had set.

As it turns out, the Mexicans were doing a "cash for keys" deal and didn't want us cutting into their money as their payout approached. With California's rental laws it takes months to kick you out of somewhere legally. If a sale was pending, and the company stood to lose money by suffering delays, they would often cash you out to the tune of a couple grand. Of course many people exploited this. In order to take advantage of this scam, all you had to do was occupy a vacant spot and have mail sent to you at that address. I knew a couple of people who did this as a matter of subsistence, moving from one to the next. I thought it was a devious way of doing things so I never tried.

Apparently, these particular Mexicans planned on taking me out of commission, keeping all of our stuff, having some rough fun with my girl and getting their several thousand dollar payout to boot. Forgive me for not feeling bad that I fouled up their plans.

It took a while for me to harden to the point where I wouldn't help just anybody. After numerous instances of being taken advantage of, squats being blown out, broken promises and stuff being stolen, I finally began to exercise a bit more caution. Even still, up until the end, I would never refuse someone food or water, even if it were my last. There were others like me, albeit only a few. Together, we were able to keep a sliver of humanity and good old-fashioned hospitality alive in that godforsaken zone.

Tragically, compassion and a kind spirit are resented, and often exploited, at every opportunity out on the streets. One has to be swift, strong and cunning in order to preserve this human decency. The paradox is, only the most violent can afford to be gentle, the weak simply can't survive its recourse.

The hardest thing about living on the streets, in my opinion, is the struggle to maintain your personal identity. It's almost impossible not to lose yourself in the swirling chaos of trying to stay alive. The crime, the violence, the hunger, the thirst, the addiction, the loss of hope, the self-loathing and the lack of self-respect are all a heavy cross to bear, but what hurt me the most was watching myself slip away.

All too easily I began to succumb to the simplistic solace of an animal existence. Nothing beyond primal needs were acknowledged because anything beyond that would often go unsatisfied. Eventually, it became easier to acknowledge defeat rather than to try to rise above it. Why grasp at straws that would only scatter when they were reached for? Anything soft and good, any weakness at all, had to be wrapped up tightly and stored away.

As I drove out these weaknesses from within myself, I became something to be feared. In doing so, I also began to lose the only thing in life that really mattered. Of what gain is "survival" if you are no longer yourself? How are you "winning" when you become all that you hate and fear? These types of thoughts made my existence loathsome beyond words. Far simpler it would have been for me to flourish in this kill-or-be-killed world had I not been plagued by who I really was deep inside, had I not been burdened by my moral compass which refused to be extinguished.

I tried so hard to embrace this darker side of myself, but when I was alone I couldn't distract myself enough. I was haunted by who I had become. These feelings were some of the darkest feelings that I have ever experienced. Sometimes, ignorance *is* bliss. What I must not discount, however, is that although these feelings created tremendous personal turmoil and were a huge disadvantage to me at the time, these feelings were also the very attributes which ultimately led to my salvation.

Gifts

The search for food and water occupied a lot of our time. In fact, access to drinking water played an important role in our selection of a place to stop or stay for a while. It's no coincidence that past civilizations centered on a water source and this remains true today as well. Most of us in our daily lives take for granted something as basic as water. I know I did.

Things are different when you are living out on the streets. Summers in central California offered weeks on end of 100-115 degree temperatures. Finding water became critical. Most business owners didn't just invite you in for a glass of water, even if you were on the verge of dying from dehydration. In fact, most would pretend not to see you in order to avoid feeling guilty or feeling compelled to help. It was just as well for me. I never was a beggar and I would have been greatly offended to be looked at as such.

Fortunately, there were actually quite a few water sources to be accessed, but like everything else, each of them carried their own risks. Most businesses had spigots located outside in the back of their buildings. Some were fenced, but not all of them. However, since water usage was monitored and the business owners were charged for its use, the cops were often called on us. Trespassing and/or theft charges were frequently pursued if we were caught drinking from them.

Another way I often got water was from the hose valve of vacant houses. The water was usually turned on in the ready-to-show or recently occupied ones. Because water is heavy you could never really carry more than a day's supply, so once a good source was found, its location was hidden, guarded and protected at all costs.

Although drinking water was of the utmost importance, water to bathe in was also a valued commodity. It didn't have to be potable or easy to transport, which made it a little easier to find, but several important factors had to be considered when choosing a site. The most important factor was security; finding a secure source was paramount.

The most vulnerable time in a person's life is, without a doubt, when bathing or using the toilet in a hostile environment. When you are homeless, your entire environment is a hostile environment and I never did either without a knife at the ready. Security implementations extended far beyond that. If I were to bathe in an empty house, I would select one that was very hard to get into. The lights would obviously be left off, all the doors and windows locked and sometimes even warning devices and/or booby traps were implemented.

The decision regarding which type of device to utilize depended on the threat level, how much time I had and what materials were available to me at that moment. A lot of times I would simply jam a spare knife into the doorframe, fashioning a hasty deadbolt of sorts. Just as often, I would hang cans or scatter broken glass to alert me of a breach. Sometimes, if it were dark outside and the approach to the house was thick with vegetation, I would hang fishhooks to snag on a potential intruder's clothing or skin.

If I were in a location that I needed to fortify due to an extremely high threat level, I would use spring traps, pressure activated munitions (12 gauge shells with a roofing nail taped to them and buried) or pungi pits. The latter of which is a concealed hole dug into the ground where the bottom is lined with spikes (nails in boards, etc…) intended to impale the perpetrator. The spikes may or may not be smeared with excrement or other substances to turn wounds septic. Battery powered motion sensors (which I seemed to acquire a lot of) could also be wired to a light, a buzzer or a solenoid that would actuate a trigger bar or explosives.

All of these implementations were well worth the effort in order to safely bathe. Oh the luxury! Such a simple and almost trivial act in our normal, civilized world, but one that is of sweetest effect while living out on the streets. Like an elixir for the spirit, a balm for the soul, some soap and hot water can change everything about you. It goes so much further than just making you look more presentable or more able to blend in with mainstream society. The effect it has on your motivation and feeling of self-worth is indescribable.

It is no coincidence that while I was in the military undergoing survival, escape and evasion courses, as well as POW classes, that this very issue was addressed. We were taught the importance of hygiene, not only for its physical importance, but for the psychological aspect as well.

I discovered, both in the military as well as out on the streets, that the most important physical aspect was keeping my feet healthy. Movement is critical in both environments. The ability to move swiftly and quietly dictates not only your success, but in some cases your very survival. To be able to escape, attack and/or travel in search of food, water and negotiable goods all depended on having healthy feet. Clean socks were treated like gold out on the streets and were not easily acquired. To compensate, keeping your feet clean and dry was imperative. This was not as easy as it sounds and much time was spent on this matter.

The act of showering and grooming was also very important psychologically. In the Army we were taught that if taken POW, we were still to shave daily and keep ourselves looking and acting with military bearing. I'm not quite sure about the nuts and bolts of this, but I have found it to be very true. Hope is in short supply out on the streets and morale is typically very low. Personally speaking, my self-esteem had taken some pretty hard hits. Bathing and grooming changed that to some degree. The simple pleasure of getting clean and feeling like I *might* look good had a profound effect on my psyche.

Don't let me fool you though, it was not an indulgence that I frequently took part in. More often than not, I would quickly dive into the canal while on the move and call that good enough. In the daytime, my clothes would be dry within 15 minutes so it wasn't a big deal.

Food acquisition was a different beast in itself. Having no electricity to rely on made the storage and preparation of food extremely challenging. Ice could rarely be afforded and a dedicated trip to steal some from a hotel ice machine was usually too time consuming to be worth the effort. Most of the time, it was literally feast or famine. When food was found, it was voraciously eaten on the spot for I was always in a calorie deficit. While on the move, I primarily subsisted on dumpster food. I was a bit squeamish about it at first but I quickly learned to adjust. Pizzas were thrown out at closing and most other fast food restaurants discarded their leftovers as well. All of these items saved my life.

I consistently traveled at night to do my foraging, not only to avoid confrontation but also because my shame, to a certain degree, mandated it. In addition, I was always hunting for the next opportunity. Because criminals and substance abusers usually prefer nocturnal hours, it was a natural fit. I also felt safer. Stealthier. Swooping through the neighborhood like a quiet breeze, flitting from shadow to shadow.

The only real drawback about traveling at night was that in those neighborhoods if the police saw you out in the hours of darkness, you were probably going to get stopped. I was usually cunning enough to avoid detection, however, potential police presence was always on my radar.

Likewise, I preferred to travel light and fast, with silence as my only companion. I was unique in this respect. Most others had a group, or gang, mentality and stuck together like a pack for safety. I chose to work alone so that I could see, hear and smell things better. This also allowed me to keep my options open and to remain flexible. Agendas could change at a moment's notice depending on what presented itself and I didn't like having to explain myself to others. My instincts ran true for the most part, and any hesitation or second guessing was detrimental to my safety.

I would travel by bicycle, whenever possible, to cover more ground and to facilitate a swift escape if necessary. If I were particularly fruitful in my findings,

I would cache and conceal the goods until I could return with a means to transport them. Often times, I would fill a shopping cart and ride my bike one-handed, pulling it behind me. These were quite noisy though, so I much preferred using a bike trailer if one were available to me.

We all had our own routes that we traveled, some were common knowledge, while others were a closely guarded secret. With that said, even with these routes, random chaos was usually the order of the day. Plans made usually materialized into plans ruined. Because of this, I operated under very loose guidelines and made sure to appreciate each gift to the fullest.

For the most part, my fruits and vegetables were gathered from the dumpsters at the zoo. The animals were fed very well with high quality foods, all of which was organically grown and of nice color and shape. Even the refuse was in surprisingly good condition. Any bad spots could easily be cut off and the yield remained quite high. Lettuce, bananas, strawberries, carrots, you name it, were harvested from this location.

Furthermore, citrus fruits thrive in the Central Valley. Grapefruits, oranges and lemons were in abundance and could be found dangling from trees on just about every block. They hung heavily over the sidewalks and were found in the yards of the abandoned houses. I had also located a pomegranate tree, a peach tree and a plum tree. The locations of these special treasures I shared with no one.

Because of the heat, finding edible meat was a rarity. A nearby warehouse laboratory, which performed various tests on meat samples, occasionally awarded results. They would take random boxes from Tyson, or other manufacturers, test a small portion and then throw the rest out. If I timed it right, I could capitalize on this. Unfortunately, the window was very small. The dumpster, as well as the entire surrounding area, stank of rotted meat. It was not a chore for the faint of heart to dive in and retrieve those usable portions. Of course the meat then had to be cooked, which created yet another obstacle to overcome. It usually wasn't worth the effort.

Bags and bags of cereal could be recovered from the dumpsters behind Catholic Charities, a local food bank. Unfortunately, vermin in this part of the city were abundant. Rodents would burrow into the bags of cereal and most would have to be thrown out. Depending on the texture, the cereal would sometimes clump up where it had been urinated in, making it easier to cull out the damaged product.

Other dried and canned goods were usually found in the alley dumpsters of low-income apartment buildings. With the economy as bad as it was, people were being evicted at a frightening rate. Every time they were evicted they would just throw out what they couldn't transport. Not only did grocery items find their way to the garbage, but quite often clothes and furniture did as well.

One morning in particular, I checked one of my usual spots in the Tower District and came upon a memorable find. Someone had either been evicted, divorced or had died because their complete wardrobe was carefully laid out across the top of the dumpster. The entire lot consisted of really nice clothes in good quality and of current fashion. They were clean, pressed and still individually shrouded in plastic, the dry cleaning tags still attached. Can you imagine my joy when I noticed that they were actually my size? I immediately sequestered them and discarded all of my old, dirty clothes. For quite a while after that I was so well dressed that I didn't even appear homeless.

41

Many others would scavenge the dumpsters for recyclables. I tagged along on a route once to understand some of the ins and outs, but quickly discovered that recycling was not to my liking. It seemed much too time consuming with too little return. However, with copper prices as high as they were, I decided that I would make an exception and give that a try.

On the corner of Belmont and Yosemite, there was a large two-story house with a high-fenced yard. It had been gutted many years before and what remained was hulking shambles. I had slept within the fenced yard on occasion. It was close to all of the happenings along Belmont, yet enough out of sight to be left alone. Many months before, I had noticed that the main overhead power line coming into the structure was disconnected from the box and hanging down. The line ran from the other side of the canal to a large tree in the yard. Ever the opportunist, I thought to myself, *Now there's something worthy of the effort to recycle.*

I disconnected the support cable and let the large wire swing to the ground. I poured a glass of water on the ends and prodded them with a stick. Nothing. I thought to myself, *Yup, they shut the power off,* and got to work. It looked like I would be able to get forty or fifty pounds of copper. I quickly scaled the tree, grabbed a hold of the wire and readied my wire cutters for use. Even though the power was off, I pulled the large strands of wire apart as far as I could before cutting them. It was blowing fairly hard and both the tree and the wire were moving all over the place.

I grabbed the first strand and cut it. Instantly, I was on the ground. My heart was pounding like a crescendo of explosions and it was a good minute before I could even see again. I fell about ten feet, but I didn't feel a thing. The only thing I remember was seeing an intensely bright flash of light and hearing a sound that seemed to be issued from hell itself. After a long search I finally found my cutters, they had a hole blasted through the blade large enough to pass your finger through. That was it for me, you couldn't even get me to look at copper wire after that.

For those of us living out on the streets, the highlight of the year was the city's annual neighborhood cleanup. The scheduled dates were posted by each neighborhood and homeowners were able to pile all of their unwanted items and debris on the curb for the city to pick up. What an open-air market of treasures! In the nicer neighborhoods, fully functional items were often tossed out simply because they had upgraded. This is an absolutely magnificent situation for someone with no means. People would clean out their garages or storage units and heap the curb with treasures. Just about anything could be found. It was amazing!

It still blows my mind that, for the most part, an entire subculture is able to survive using only what is discarded by average American citizens. Unfortunately, some people are resentful of others finding use in something that they have paid money for. During my travels, I noticed a few areas where the residents would consistently throw their litter boxes on top of any food items, without fail. They would also deliberately slash any clothing to render it unusable. Nonetheless, I always felt that these displays of self-serving bitterness were the exception rather than the rule.

To satisfy my sweet tooth, I hit up the dumpsters behind the battered woman's shelter. I would routinely harvest dozens of cakes and pies, almost more than I could carry. At the Mexican donut shop, they would leave the donuts that they pulled after rotating their stock at the top of their dumpster. If I arrived before it had been rooted through, quite a few meals could be secured in one swoop. Of course they consisted of only carbohydrates and sugars, but somehow they kept me going for a good stretch of time.

I remember one day quite vividly. I was hungry, ravenously hungry. The sun was high in the sky bearing down furiously on any of us foolhardy enough to be out in it. I was so tired that it was all I could do to keep trudging on. My senses were dulled by the heat and pure exhaustion. I felt almost as if I were wrapped up tightly in a husk that I could only vaguely see or hear out of. The quiet words, *I'm so hungry,* had become a scream in my head as the hours wore on. I was so frustrated and miserable that I literally wanted to cry. Alone and starving, I had nowhere to go and absolutely nothing to look forward to. My mind was horribly numbed by this abuse. Stoically, I put one foot in front of the other, over and over and over again.

Eventually, I passed by the Mexican bakery. Because it was well into the day, I knew that it was long past time to be able to forage food from the dumpster. Dejected, I kept walking. As I passed by I noticed a pastry bag delicately perched on the rim, shimmering in the sun. Denying hope, I walked up to investigate. Bracing for the inevitable crushing reality of an empty bag, I reached for it. Fresh out of the oven, purchased and left for whatever reason, was an enormous apple fritter. I carefully took it and sprinted away to a small stand of trees further down the alley. There, in shade and privacy, I ate it. Crumb by precious crumb, I savored this delectable morsel until not one bite remained.

It's amazing, really, how one little pastry was able to change everything. I was so happy that I bubbled with laughter. With my belly content, I slaked my thirst with a long draught of water from the spigot behind the store and then stretched out and enjoyed 3/4 of a discarded cigarette from the veranda floor of a bar down the street.

Whether a random act of kindness, a gift from God or just the universe's chaos falling in my favor, I'll never know. What I do know is that I'll never forget that day. It sparked a small change in me. From then on, no matter how bad things got, I knew that I was going to be ok. Because I knew this, it was so. I can never truly articulate the power of the emotions I felt that day. The despair. The triumph. What I can convey, however, is what it culminated in. Insight. Perspective. Truth. May every experience bring us these gifts.

The Smell of Truth

There really are monsters out there, and in this particular neighborhood they were out in full force. It didn't seem so bad by day, but those of us who lived there knew better. After dark it was a constant free-for-all. The area was so grimy that even lower level predators steered clear for fear of things that go bump in the night. My companion and I had been separated for a bit leading up to this. I don't recall the exact reason, but it doesn't really matter for we were separated often. Somebody had to hit the licks and barter to support our habits, and that somebody was usually me.

We came upon each other one night and she excitedly told me of an abando that she had arranged for us to stay in. She had agreed to care for the girlfriend of The Block Monster, who was an acquaintance of ours. Apparently, he had broken his girlfriend's leg during one of their fights. She was bedridden and couldn't care for herself so Nashelle agreed to help keep her safe, cook and score drugs for her while she healed. In exchange for this care, we were allowed a room of our own to stay in. This meant that we were also able to lock up our gear while we were away. What freedom!

I was excited for this opportunity, however, I should have trusted my instincts. Clanging warning bells were going off in my head as we approached. An unshakable sense of dread and desolate despair permeated the area and seemed to creep into my very soul.

As I always do upon entry, I cleared the house with a large hunting knife at the high ready. After doing so, I checked the grounds and walked the fence line, noting all access and egress points. This practice has served me quite well over the years. On the streets, you never trust somebody's word that a place is safe, in fact, you must assume the opposite.

For security purposes, I liked the high fence that surrounded the house and the accompanying yard. I loosened two boards first thing to ensure that we had an escape route to the alley if necessary. Another thing that I liked in the backyard was a fairly large shed with a small storage loft inside. I found it to be a good fallback position and noted that it would also be a good watch position for the house. A lot of times, when I returned to wherever I was staying, I would creep soundlessly to a vantage point to look, listen, and "feel" before clearing and entering.

One thing that struck me as odd about this particular shed were the old, rusty hasps on the outside of the barred windows and the big heavy door. The large rusty meat hooks hanging from chains within the shed also caught my eye. Although these noted observations seemed odd, I didn't give them much thought at the time. In hindsight, I believe I may have downplayed these features due to the fact that I was so happy to get inside and get off my feet for a bit.

Time isn't as relevant on the streets. Days seem to blur into one continuous, discombobulated mess, so I couldn't really tell you how long we were there before we got word that The Block Monster had been picked up by the police while on a foraging trip. It wasn't too much longer that his girlfriend's leg turned horribly septic.

We didn't have any electricity or running water at the house. Because of this, you couldn't even open the bathroom door without gagging. The toilet was horribly plugged and heaped with excrement and the bathtub was caked with something that looked even worse. Her infected leg could be smelled even above this horrid stench. We were finally able to persuade her to reach out to her family and seek medical attention before she lost her leg altogether.

With her gone, we felt a little more comfortable moving about the house. She had requested that we stay there in her absence to watch over the place and we were more than happy to oblige. It felt great to stop jumping around and to settle in for a bit. We cleaned up the house as best as we could, made sure that security was up to par and then concentrated on fixing up our room and squaring away our gear. My companion, who had the heart of a gypsy, happily turned our room into a tiny magical kingdom, skillfully applying her touches of craft and décor.

The windows were blacked out heavily so as to not betray our presence, but inside they were furled with lace curtains and colorful scarves. A mirror adorned one wall and plants were carefully set in the corners of the room. Our gear, once unpacked and repacked, was stowed in our room's closet. The bed was made using our unzipped sleeping bags. Several candles bathed the room in a soft, dancing light. A makeshift washtub was at the foot of the bed and we quietly bathed each other with tender attention before we lay together to sleep. She was so beautiful in the light and we clung to each other fiercely. We were oblivious to all of the pain and evil that permeated the grounds only yards away from us.

At that time, nothing else mattered. So cold. So hungry. So tired. So alone. So scared. So devoid of hope. In that moment I clung to her with a need that surpassed any hunger I have ever known. She met my ache with her own, and together we explored the heavens. It was always like that with her. Knowing that we were not promised tomorrow, we lived and loved as such. We continued in this manner for about three days, gracing our bodies and our souls with a closeness that you can never have on the streets.

On the third night, I heard a noise in the yard so I grabbed my knife and crept to the back of the house to ambush whoever was stealing on us. To my surprise, it was The Block Monster himself and he had brought us food. He was a very intense man but we were similar in some respects so we carried an uneasy truce. He ran solo, just like me, in gang-held neighborhoods that didn't allow much margin for error. He was also a former Marine and we often talked shop. We comfortably shared intel on where we were operating, who was doing what, who was buying or selling, who was good or bad, etc…. There was, however, one thing that really disturbed me about him. The glint of madness that I saw deep within his eyes indicated that he wasn't just a little crazy like me, but crazy to a level that actually scared me.

I set this fear to the side as best as I could because out on the streets an insane ally is much better than one with a more conventional grasp of reality. Someone who doesn't have any limits, who's unpredictable and goes "all in" without really thinking of consequences is a good person to have on your side. He liked the rumors that I had beaten a serial rapist nearly to death with a hammer, and I liked his reputation, so we got along well.

When he came to us that day with food, I didn't register anything more than a pleasant surprise. It wasn't just food, it was meat! It wasn't just meat, it was fresh meat! Acquiring meat that wasn't spoiled from the brutal California sun was definitely an infrequent treasure. We were more than happy to accept the three or four pounds of newspaper-wrapped steaks and roasts that he presented to us. The smell was a bit unique, but we seasoned it heavily and greedily ate this precious gift. It had been many weeks since we had consumed meat.

It was probably a week or two later before I saw him again. He had really worked himself into a frenzy about something and was a total mess. We went inside the house to parley. After he calmed down we cross-loaded our weapons and equipment. We were both sickened to the deepest parts of our being about the current state of our world. Girls were disappearing and being found in dumpsters, raped and butchered. Kids were being shot and killed for no reason other than standing in front of the wrong house at the wrong time. And so on, and so forth.

I'd had many attempts on my own life made by this time and I was tired of being perceived as a possible target. I wanted to start changing things. We both did. We talked for hours about how scared we were for the people that we loved; how scared we were for ourselves. We discussed the fact that there was so much evil in the world that people no longer attempted to resist it, how some people actually reveled in savaging

51

and abusing those who were weaker than them. We agreed that nothing was sacred anymore, how nobody even knew what love or respect meant.

It was only after we had shed all of those tears of pain and helpless rage together that he told me that he was an angel. He believed that I had also been chosen and that we were to use our God-given talents towards the fulfillment of the divine purpose, the purpose in which we had been born. He noted that the words "strength" and "honor" on my arms clearly marked me as a fulfillment of his prophecy.

Fulfillment of the divine purpose? What? Thinking to myself how preposterous this was, I found myself in a panic. He was clearly out of his mind. Knowing that I had to outwardly stay cool, I frantically began to internally process every nuance of his behavior. It was then that he entrusted me to become part of his holiest ritual. He wanted to show me how he prayed, and for me to pray with him. We knelt beside each other on the living room floor and he led us in prayer as the waning light of the afternoon sun streamed in and painted our tear-streaked faces.

He asked God for the blessing, might and power to not shrink or draw back from the task that was appointed to us. We bowed to the floor and as we did so I almost wretched from the rotted stench that came up from the carpet. We lifted our heads and he asked for strength and swiftness to be bestowed upon us. Again, we bowed to the floor. Again, I almost wretched, now horrified from the smell. We lifted our heads and he asked to be reserved a place at the right hand, for this was the hand of vengeance and the hammer of truth. A third and final time we bowed to the floor. My forehead on the carpet, choking to swallow my vomit, I watched him out of the corner of my eye. Every nerve in my body was screaming for me to leave.

In that moment, I was as scared as I have ever been in my entire life. I didn't know exactly *what* was wrong, but I knew *something* was wrong. It took every ounce of my strength to not get up and run out of that house. Here I was, bowing to the floor in an execution-style pose, defying all of my previous training and logic with regards to never turning my back on my enemy. His intentions were still unclear to me but his sinister tone had me on high alert. I knew that I had to play this out, for my only advantage would be the element of surprise.

Finally, after what felt like an eternity, we raised our heads and rose to our feet. Looking deep into my eyes, he hugged me tightly and told me that he had work to do. He casually warned me to stay out of a particular area of the city and I awkwardly told him that his carpet smelled like he had rubbed it with a dead dog. He looked at me with a distant look and said, "That's the smell of truth." With that, he turned and walked away, never once looking back.

It was only a couple of days later that I heard the news. Allegedly, two teens had tried to rob him at a seedy hotel that we all frequented for business. It was reported that he calmly shot both of them in the face and carried them to the dumpster, where he threw them in a heap. He was sentenced to life in prison. I also heard from several witnesses that the kids didn't attempt to rob him at all, that they were good kids who had been gunned down in cold blood "just for kicks". There were rumors that he was responsible for many more disappearances. Whispers of cannibalism were also circulating. I immediately flashed back to the eerie shed with the meat hooks and the foul smelling carpet. It made me sick to my stomach.

I will never know for sure what I ate that day all wrapped up in newspaper. I will also never know for sure why the house smelled like a butcher shop stewed by the hot sun and why the carpet smelled like dead animal had been rubbed into it. That's the way I want it. Nonetheless, I do know several things to be true. I know that I looked straight into the eyes of death that day, but for some reason I was spared. I also know that I experienced a real life case study of a psychopath on a personal level. Even more disturbing, I know that he saw something in me that he felt was the same as in him.

What did he see? What was it about me that made him feel like we were teammates of some sort, like we shared a kinship? This disturbed me on the deepest level, however, more than likely it was this very belief that saved my life. I learned from this experience that sometimes your closest acquaintance can become your biggest liability. This lesson cemented the fact that, on the streets, you can trust no one.

As disturbed as I was by the discovery that he felt that we were both equals, I was also comforted by the fact that I knew, deep down, that we were not. I couldn't be. During our prayer, I feared and prayed and hoped that I wouldn't have to kill him, but was preparing to do so if necessary. I knew that I wouldn't enjoy killing him. Because of this, I knew we were not the same.

Robin Hood

Although no one could be trusted, and it was definitely an "every man for himself" type of mentality out on the streets, there was also a strange sense of unity between its inhabitants. Things were so tough that there was almost a sense of civic pride between those of us who lived there. Although each of us was clearly out for ourselves most of the time, we did look out for each other to a certain extent. It was almost an "us against them" mentality, with us, being the poor and downtrodden, versus them, the rest of the world.

I personally had a Robin Hood romanticism attached to my outlook. I once handed out stacks of laptops to people who would otherwise never have them. Another time I passed out a shopping cart full of Enfamil formula to single mothers in the hood. I gave away mounds of food whenever I had a surplus. I provided people a change of clothes when running from the cops. Many times. We all did this. It was our duty to those in the hood.

In particular, I always looked out for the youngsters and tried to spit positive truths to them whenever I could. That's what an OG is supposed to do. The term OG, translated literally, means original gangster. In many organizations it is used to denote the "shot callers", but not always. Amongst the Bulldogs, it was simply a term used for older, experienced and proven gangsters. Some, such as myself, were referred to as an OG based strictly on personal conduct and were called that out of respect.

Although I interacted with active members of many organizations and kept abreast of policies, politics and current events, I have never been a member of any gang or criminal organization. I have sworn allegiance only to my God, my family and the principles of my country's founding. With that said, being called an OG by the young gang members who all knew that I was independent made me very proud. It meant that what I said was weighed as valid and that my conduct was honorable and worthy of respect.

Having earned their respect, I took advantage of this by trying to help the youngsters as much as I could. They didn't know what I knew. They had convinced themselves, or at least tried to, that they were tough gangsters. They weren't fooling me. I knew that they were scared just like everybody else. On their own, they were pretty harmless. It wasn't until they were in a group that they would pump each other up enough to hurt or kill someone.

I taught them many skills that I know, without a doubt, kept them alive. I showed them things that changed their entire outlook, but then again, they did the same for me. When it comes down to it, we are all the same in that regard. Each perspective is relevant and of worth. Those of us who have learned things, in my opinion, must be compelled to share these personal truths. Much the same, we must all learn to value the knowledge gifted to us by others as well.

On one occasion, a few weeks after being forced out of the garage, I returned to The Trap to conduct some business. I was about halfway through the transaction when I heard "Got you now!" I turned in time to see three Bulldog gang members coming at me with knives. I heard two or three more coming around the side of the house. In a flash, I dove out the window and sprinted down the street. I could hear their feet pounding in pursuit behind me and it spurred me to an even greater effort. I knew the young kid who was closest behind me. He was fast, but I was able to shake him by running through yards and leaping over fences. I ran until my legs could no longer carry me and my lungs felt like they were about to burst.

Weeks later, as I came across each of them independently, we smoked a cigarette and laughed about how I was the fastest white boy on two feet. I joked about how they would all be some stone-cold killers, if only they weren't so darn slow. There were no hard feelings between us. With that said, we all knew that if they would have caught me that day, they would have killed me.

Sometime later I gave the youngster, who was almost close enough to get a knife in me, a machete when he was having some problems with rival gangsters. Not the brightest of moves, I suppose, but I could see the respect in their eyes at these displays of machismo that I offered to them. At the time, I really needed something to feel good about.

Of course things didn't always go so well. One night in particular, while I was staying in the garage at The Trap, it went very badly. It had been cold out, so when one of the young Bulldog gang members asked me for a coat, I was happy to oblige. The coat and hat that I had been wearing that day were right by the door. I handed them over and asked that he return them when he was finished. About an hour later he came running along the rooftops across the alley, jumped down and ran through the yard. He quickly shed the hat and coat and threw them at me, running off into the darkness.

I was awakened less than an hour later by a loud pounding on my door. Wearing only my boxers, I grabbed my machete and opened it. The muzzles of two nine millimeters greeted me, and the faces of the cops behind them were stern. They asked me where I had been earlier that night and said they needed to search the place. NOW. The incredulous look on my face as they overlooked the drugs and paraphernalia, stolen goods and 12 gauge ammo, prompted a response from them. "We're looking for a murder weapon, a .44 magnum," said one. They completed their search, found nothing and left after informing me that a detective would be in touch.

Apparently, the kid who had borrowed my clothes had shot somebody in the face with a .44 magnum less than a block away from The Trap. This was his attempt at setting me up. So yeah, sometimes people really do spit in your face when you do something nice for them.

I didn't help others to gain respect or to be considered the "top dog" of the hood. I did it because I was just trying to be decent. Unfortunately, this created a big problem for me. Because I was becoming so highly revered among those who were weaker than me, I was also becoming a threat to those in positions of power out on the streets. So, in a sense, I was gaining respect from some, but earning resentment from others for the very same actions. There were quite a few times when situations escalated out of control. In these cases,

I consorted with the Bulldog OGs to help make these problems go away.

Interestingly enough, old school gang etiquette and machismo demanded exaggerated manhood. Most important issues went unspoken. Agreements were never clearly worded. Assets were treated as if they meant nothing. The greater the gift or sacrifice given, the more noble you were. Weaknesses were not acknowledged; it was understood that none of us had any. If I had a problem on the block because I carried myself as friendly, fair and honest, yet capable of and with a propensity for extreme violence, my voice was heard when I came to the them.

I was definitely very mindful about how I approached the OGs, as there was most certainly a process. In a time-honored fashion, I would open with formal pleasantries. Then, we would smoke together. After we had done this (and even if I were in a hurry and it was excruciating hard to do so), I would slowly weave the conversation towards whatever issue I was plagued with. I would keep things offhand and relatively vague, making light of any hardship or calamity I had endured. When the picture was painted to my satisfaction, I would then present gifts: laptops, bullet proof vests, knives, you know, the normal "gangster swag".

After these gifts were (nonchalantly) handed over, I would make an offhand remark as to how my problem might go away (but no big deal if it didn't). I would assure them that I could get through anything. "Yes, yes," we would agree as we had a parting smoke, "there's nothing we can't handle." Most times, it was as if I had wished my problem away while sharing small talk and a good smoke with a friend. This just goes to show that even in today's self-centered world, a little respect can go a long way in some circles.

American Flags & Bulldozers

Eventually, after repeated abuse, there comes a point when you stop trusting people altogether. This is exactly what happened to us. We had been on the streets for quite a while by this point and we were tired of dealing with troublesome people. Camping seemed like the next obvious choice. There were a few homeless camps already in place, but crime permeated these menagerie of hovels and huts and they were rife with filth and decay. Being congested and overpopulated, it took one glance for me to know that it wasn't the right place for us.

Initially, we camped in various places in solitary, frequently moving around. Although our interactions with people were more limited, the moving around part was tiring so we set out in search of a more permanent location. We ended up at a small, partially hidden campsite located next to the railroad tracks between Olive and Belmont streets. There was about fifteen feet between the tracks and a thick, unending hedge of oleanders. Our campsite was in-between the two.

Every so often a freight train would rush through in a roaring, clattering, cacophony of sound and motion. We could feel it through the ground and all of our senses were inundated with this assault. As if that weren't enough, they would blast their horn in long, powerful, notes due to the numerous crossings nearby. Fortunately, it didn't take long to become deadened to this constant racket.

The residents across the street appeared to be just as acclimated, for they rarely looked twice in our direction. We carefully concealed our camp from view to avoid disturbing or offending them. For a while we were left alone. As time passed, more and more homeless were drawn to the area. Unfortunately, most of them weren't as conscientious about their visible impact. A fair amount of them recycled for income so large piles of refuse were in mounds around their areas. There were others who had obviously never heard of the expression "don't shit where you eat".

These newcomers ruined it for all of us by targeting homes and garages in the immediate area for theft and vandalism. Their ignorance painted each and every one of us in a bad light. Tension and discord began to mount between the residents and the homeless. Each day contained some form of confrontation. I felt very ashamed that these newcomers were victimizing the residents who had, up until this point, treated us with indifference and sometimes even kindness. I also felt angry that our entire group was being measured by the actions of a careless few.

It wasn't long before the police were sweeping through our camp a couple of times per day and I was hauled in repeatedly for minor infractions. The worst part about being picked up was that on most occasions my companion had no idea what had happened to me. I was horribly frustrated and worried about her being alone in that cesspool. Each time I got out, usually only a few days or weeks later, I would track her down only to find that our stuff had been ransacked or that she had moved because she'd been attacked. All of these factors made my decision for finding a better site imperative.

About two miles down the tracks was a fledgling homeless community. It was in the same type of squalor, however, it was in an older industrial section of town. Its location, and the fact that everybody was more out of sight, made police presence much less of an issue. Contact with residents was also greatly decreased so there was a lot less friction in that respect as well. We hauled our belongings down there, staked a claim, and set up camp. I had procured a brand new twelve man tent which became the center of our camp. I decked it out with a futon mattress and hung curtains between the different areas and over the doorway. A matching bed set was draped over the mattress and couch.

We lived there only a few months before things went sour. One of the nearby warehouse owners decided to expand his property line and we were all in his path. Our backs to the canal already, we tore up the order to vacate and obstinately declined. The next day a work crew came and started fencing in our encampment. We were told that everything would be bulldozed upon completion of the fence. Each night, after the work crew left, I would tear down the days progress and throw the posts and fencing into the canal. Each day, they came and replaced it, getting a little farther each time. After several days of this, things finally reached a breaking point.

The next day, when the work crew arrived, there was an additional crew with them. These guys did not work on the fence. Instead, they took positions along the perimeter, encircling us. Their steely eyes and the bulges at their waistband told me what their job was. I responded in kind. I made four Molotov cocktails, put them in a pack, strapped on my machete and went to work myself. I moved outside the perimeter and outside the area that we were to be contained in. Back and forth, in random, erratic patterns I moved and moved and moved.

When you are faced with superior numbers, movement is key. The goal is to turn your opposition's masses into a liability. The strength of this crew's force now meant nothing to me since I had negated their position by eliminating a front. I was all around them. Between them. Behind them. I harassed and goaded as I went. Mocking and laughing at them, trying to lure them into committing to a course of action.

Word of this volatile situation had gotten out and it wasn't long before the entire area was swamped with news crews and staff from various agencies. City and county agencies, homeless advocates, a VA rep and a HUD rep were all there. There must have been four different news crews in all. I must admit, it really was a piece of dramatic journalism, us taking down our American flag while our homes were being bulldozed.

If you look closely, you'll notice that most major homeless communities proudly display the American flag. Most of those who do are veterans, but sometimes others hang them as well to remind the public that this is America, and that the homeless are Americans too. I've even seen it hung upside down at a few sites, not as a sign of disrespect, but as an official distress signal.

The fact that this incident was resolved without violent action, in my opinion, was only because of all of the attention drawn. Most of the people in our group weren't proactive and lost everything once the bulldozers eventually came through. I made sure that my companion and I weren't a statistic. We hadn't many options on where to go so we hauled our stuff across the canal using the nearby railway bridge. There was a no-man's-land of sorts over there. Private property, city property, county property and railroad property all converged in that one area and nobody was exactly sure of each boundary. Because of this uncertainty, no single agency felt compelled to act against our staying there.

It was a barren, dusty, wind-swept and sunbaked strip of land. There had been camps there before, once upon a time, but an arsonist had leveled them and they had long been in disuse. We cleaned the area well and quickly made it our home. Warehouses bordered one side, railroad tracks another, the canal composed the third border and the HWY 180 overpass made up the last. There was a business about a quarter of a mile away that had an external spigot for drinking water and the canal was suitable for our bathing and washing needs.

In the beginning, there were only three sites set up. My companion and I spearheaded the settling of the area and placed our site along the canal. We started off in small tents but quickly modified our living arrangements to that which resembled the quarters of a Bedouin chieftain. The tents, with no airflow, were just too stifling in the wicked Fresno heat.

We erected main poles and ran ropes between them and staked them off under tension. These were about twelve feet tall. We covered these with layers and layers of tarps, pulled tight and staked so that the edges were about three feet off of the ground. Both the layers and the airflow were critical to cope with the heat. It would typically be 115 degrees for weeks on end in the summer. With no AC or ice, and water in limited supply, construction techniques were critical and were continually adjusted as we learned more about desert survival.

I ringed the compound with tangled brush and logs and erected palm fronds along the outskirts of this for privacy screening. This fence was needed, not only to keep the voracious wild dogs out of our food stockpiles, but to deter thieves as well. In no time at all, we had eight or nine camping tents which were erected around the perimeter. These allowed for people to stay for short periods of time. They were almost like rentals but with the agreement being much less formal. We helped others with a place to stay while they figured out what they were going to do next. In return, we asked for them to help us however they were able to. They could get us water or ice, provide cigarettes, donate food, get us high, etc....

Our personal quarters were indeed something to behold. In the jumbled absurdity of it all, much like an abstract painting, beauty was found in the contrast and irregularity of not only the rudimentary character, but periodically in its metaphorical use.

Comfort wasn't exclusively found in tangible items. Sometimes comfort was measured by the glint of sunlight allowed through a gap in our structure, or appreciated in a small piece of wood or stone that reminded me of somewhere far removed from then and there. Sometimes it was a smell that hinted of a life long gone, or a child's toy that whispered to me of dreams long shattered. Sometimes comfort meant my triple stacked futon mattresses, dressed with a pillow top comforter and fitted with satin sheets. None of it made sense, but it all made sense. In such a life where possessions were transient at best, the very worth of things became what they triggered within me, not the items themselves.

With that said, my general preference in decor favored clean lines and open simplicity. Most of my things lent themselves towards a practical nature, however, I rather enjoyed transcending the parameters of what standards were expected of me as a homeless man. I chose to view my lack of walls or a roof as a blank palette to work with. Limited only by my personal imagination and creativity, I would time and again exceed the sum of the materials and tools at hand and defy reason with the things that I created.

One of my accomplishments was a multi-level deck area with sleeping platforms and a sitting area. The fact that this area was raised meant that we caught more of the afternoon breeze to cool ourselves. It also elevated us so that we were out of reach of the swarms of fire ants that inhabited our area. Additionally, it gave us a better vantage point to survey all of the access routes into camp with our field glasses, or binoculars. We would draw back from the openings as a sniper would, never betraying our position but always forewarned of approaching trouble.

There were many benefits to communal living. For one, it felt really good to know that we wouldn't have to leave at a moment's notice. Truth be told, it was all temporary, but it still felt like home. Tasks could be shared and information could be passed back and forth. It also changed the nature of our foraging trips. We were able to repair and put into use many of the items that we found. Area rugs, end tables, couches, recliners, dressers for our clothes, racks for our shoes, toolboxes and totes for tools were all brought home.

Citronella tiki torches lit the yard area and our personal quarters were always bathed in light from various candles and oil lamps. I even found a neon light tube used for mounting underneath cars that I hooked up to a large RV battery. It was bright enough to make the entire camp look like a rave. Not exactly great for staying low key, but sometimes it was fun to be festive and playful. One of our more extravagant luxuries was a small kiddie pool which was rigged with a misting device that I fashioned from a 12-volt windshield washer pump and some tubing which ran into the canal. This definitely helped keep us comfortable during the stifling hot summers.

Having a more permanent campsite also meant that we were able to stockpile canned goods and other dried food items. Racks, screens and bricks were drug back to construct a wood-fired BBQ and pizza oven. I threw down some awesome ribs in my pit when I was able to. The only drawback of preparing food under these conditions was that cleanup was such a hassle. Most of the time we kept things pretty simple. Our camp was adjacent to a dairy producer, so occasionally we were blessed with a jug of milk. Sometimes, I think they would drop them on purpose and set it out by the dumpster. Who knows, but God bless them if they did.

A lot of people had food stamps, or EBT as it's called these days. Around the first of the month I would usually trade drugs or other negotiable items for some real food. I personally didn't receive unemployment, section eight, EBT or any other type of charity handout. When my backpack was stolen, and my wallet with it, my options became quite limited. Just about every assistance program out there hinges upon first presenting identification.

When our original camp was bulldozed, I missed out on the opportunity for assistance from HUD because of this very reason, I didn't have either an ID or my DD214 papers from the military. Still, even if I would have had an ID, I'm not sure if my pride would have allowed me to receive any sort of handout at the time. It's for that very reason that I never went out to "spange", or post up at intersections and ask for spare change, as others did. It just wasn't for me.

The problem of not having an ID sounds like such a simple problem to remedy. However, it was daunting to someone in my position. First, the logistics hindered me. Getting to the DMV early enough to be helped was often a challenge since all of my scavenging was done at night. California DMVs aren't like your average DMV location. You will easily wait in line for seven or eight hours if an appointment is not secured beforehand. Additionally, coming up with the cash for the fees was rarely attainable.

After passing all of these hurdles, the difficulty was not even close to being over. I still had to prove who I was, and with no supporting identification and no means of getting any, that was next to impossible. Nor did I have an address or phone number, both of which were necessary. With identity theft running rampant, they were quite stringent about their policies. I suppose I could have been more persistent, but after failing on my first four attempts to get an ID card, it really started to seem impossible. In addition, if I actually had a few dollars at that point, it was hard to choose anything other than food to spend it on.

In retrospect, it seems odd to me that while living in this homeless community I enjoyed some of my most memorable meals. Most of it was swill of course, absolute spoiled filth, but every once in a while there was a diamond in the rough. Truth be told, I had the best turkey of my life while living there.

First, we lined a shopping cart with bricks. The bottom tier was in a single layer, and the top tier included the bottom as well as the sides. A fire was stoked underneath the cart and was cared for throughout the day. The bricks became hot and held a consistent temperature. On the top layer we laid a saucer-like liner from a raised patio fire pit. In this, we placed the large turkey, which we slathered with butter and beer and seasoned with garlic, salt and pepper. We stuffed it with onions, which is all we had, and then covered it with a huge wok which I had scavenged from the dumpster at a Chinese restaurant. The wok was much larger than the fire pit saucer beneath it and when turned upside down, it caused the smoke to roll over the turkey the entire time it was cooking.

Nashelle tended the fire and continually basted the bird as it slowly cooked and smoked the nine or so hours that I was at work. I will remember that meal for as long as I live. It was the most succulent, flavorful fowl that I have ever eaten. Anytime. Anywhere. I find it amazing that such incredible results were rendered from a shopping cart smoker. This certainly proves that where there is a will, there is most definitely a way.

Once our camp was constructed to our satisfaction, we were finally able to relax a bit and enjoy a few hobbies. I was always procuring and fashioning weapons. Most I sold or traded. Some I kept. All were tested. I found that I had quite a knack for throwing axes; much time was spent in constructing the perfect design for my particular throwing style. I masterfully completed the ideal combination and ended up using it for quite a while. A log round was placed on its side by the doorway and I would spend hours burying my tomahawk into it. From my bed. From the kitchen area. From my chair. From anywhere and everywhere. It's no coincidence that I knew the exact range to the doorway from every corner of my abode.

I would also make jewelry and tinker with various projects so there was always something of interest laying around our quarters. It was really quite comfortable. It was our home. I did the best I could to thwart the ever present dust and sand, the brutal heat and the fierce indigenous insects. Each of these challenges were circumvented and new ones met. In a way, the adversity was good for me. It kept my mind busy. It kept me moving forward. Each little battle that I won, no matter how insignificant, was still a victory. And I needed that.

Although everyday life was looking up, holidays were pretty awful. Simply put, they were just another grim reminder that we were different. That we were less. That we had nothing. That we were worth nothing. They reminded us of the people that we had lost and of the lives that we had failed. Violent crimes usually spiked and substance abuse rose to a peak on these days. Most everyone was irritable and miserable. As I slipped further and further from mainstream life, I came to loathe the holidays more and more.

If I wanted to send a girl into uncontrollable sobbing, all I had to do was give her a rose on Valentine's Day. Acts of kindness and normalcy are so foreign on the streets that they almost become too overwhelming to take, the reminder of our former lives simply too much to handle. This kind of pain touched everyone, the strong and the weak. No one was exempt. In addition, most stores and other businesses were closed so our general patterns were disrupted. There was also a heavier police presence due to the increase in DUI checkpoints. It's easy to see why none of us cared for these "special occasions". I suppose the only exception would be Halloween. I would typically cavort about the entire month of October in a Jason mask. Good times, right?

The only other holiday that appeared to be celebrated amongst those of us who inhabited the streets was New Year's Eve. Typically, at about 11:30 pm, everyone would empty their guns into the sky as the city's fireworks bathed the night in flashes and earth-shaking explosions. It was a chilling reminder of how much firepower was out on the streets during this "mad minute". Every type of weapon, in every caliber, could be heard during this sobering display of rebellion. It really did sound like the war zone that it was. Some of us called it "the killing time" because even the police would lock down during those last few minutes of the year. Once, I had been picked up on New Year's Eve for outstanding warrants and the cops refused to take me to central booking until the ferocious hail of gunfire was over. We sat safely locked in a small substation until I was finally able to start my new year in the Fresno County Jail, or County, as we called it.

The advantages of the community were many, but human nature would invariably rear its ugly head. There was always some kind of fracas or discord amongst us. It was common for others to become resentful if you appeared happy or comfortable. They would covet not only your belongings, but your pleasantries as well.

Camps were routinely razed and our camp was no exception. To some extent, we stood together. We would look out for each other's stuff and have each other's backs in simple matters, but disagreements that stemmed from something trivial could quickly escalate into a beating or fatality, and often did. For this reason most just minded their own business. It was a community, but it was a lawless community. All alone and out of sight, when it really came down to it, the only one there who could protect you, was you.

Not-So-Small Miracles

When you are sick and weak, the bad guys don't just go away. In fact, that's usually when they strike. Life on the streets is hard enough when you are feeling your best, but when you're sick or injured, it really puts you in a life-threatening and vulnerable position. I've been in several situations where nothing short of a miracle has saved me. Normally, I rely on my strength, my street smarts and my tactical skills and training to protect myself, but on those particular occasions, these attributes were simply not enough. It took divine intervention, in one form or another, to keep me alive. These occurrences also illustrate the true testament of my body's will to survive.

Sometimes, miracles come in the form of small, unexpected packages.

I hadn't been to the dentist in years. One of the unfortunate side effects of both meth use, as well as homelessness, is that one's teeth will fall into an onerous state of disrepair. My teeth had also suffered numerous impacts from wrecks and fights so they were in a very fragile state. Of course it was only a matter of time until an infection set in. At this time, we were living beside the tracks near the oleander hedgerow. We had a tiny pup tent for shelter. In that heat, when you climbed inside, you felt like you had been shrink-wrapped. It was unbearably hot.

One of my upper teeth had developed an abscess and it wasn't long before my face had swollen to the point where I thought it would split open. I grew lethargic and weak and within a couple of days I could only stand up or move around for a couple of minutes before exhaustion set in. I would crawl miserably into that tiny little furnace of a tent and fade in and out of consciousness. I didn't have a remedy for the pain, and soon it was all I knew. Blackness and pain.

During this time, we had a reindeer Chihuahua named Sasha. She was the sweetest and smartest little creature I have ever known. We were very fond of each other and spent quite a lot of time in each other's company. As I lay there, out of my mind with pain and too weak to push her away, the strangest thing happened. My face was stretched so swollen and tight that I couldn't tell what she was doing at first. I couldn't feel it. As I slowly emerged from the fog, I came to realize that she had her entire muzzle inside my mouth and was licking the shattered remnants of my bad tooth. Afterwards, she forced herself upon me, and like a tiny little anteater, shot her tongue up my nose and into my sinus cavity to address the rest of the infected area.

At first I tried to object to this obtrusive violation of my dignity. I pushed her away. *Why wouldn't she let me suffer in peace,* I thought, *why did she refuse to let me die like a man?* Instead, she seemed intent on humiliating me in (what I thought were) my final hours. Every time I regained consciousness, I found her in the midst of one of her assaults. Before long, I was weakened to the point where I just let her do what she wanted to do. Strangely enough, I began to feel better. The pressure eventually began to go away and the pain subsided. Still, every time I awoke she was feverishly going to work on my afflicted area. Amazingly, I felt stronger. It didn't hurt anymore. There wasn't any more swelling. That little dog saved my life!

Perhaps dogs have some kind of special enzyme in their saliva that either kills bacteria or promotes healing. I don't know, but I'll always feel like she did something really special for me that day as I lay there waiting to die. I feel a bit sheepish even telling this tale, but I owe her. She was hit by a car a couple of months later. I really struggled with this loss. Her love, devotion and hard work had saved me. I wish I could have done the same for her.

Sometimes, miracles come in the form of kindness.

I'm sure that the effects of a massive staphylococcus infection are grievous, but in my condition they were almost the end of me. Of course I had been up for weeks. I was malnourished, dehydrated and just overall in really bad shape. I knew exactly when it happened. A nasty gash on my left shin had been giving me some trouble, but it had finally scabbed over and was healing nicely. Because it was no longer an open wound, I wasn't as concerned about keeping it covered.

It was sweltering out, and I was wearing a pair of baggy khaki shorts and nothing else. I had been riding my bike and saw someone that I knew, so I veered over and skidded to a stop. As I stood and straddled my bike, the handlebars flopped over. As it did so, the front tire grazed my leg and ripped off my scab. I had just ridden down the edge of the street, so my wound was instantly smeared with foul, muddy, gutter water. *That's not good*, I thought, but I didn't dwell on it as I carried on about my evening.

By the next morning my lower leg was twice its normal size. Angry red streaks consumed my leg and sprawled out farther and farther from the epicenter. Racked with fever and bone shaking chills, I sought out Nashelle. I hadn't seen her for a while but held out hope that she would still help me. I couldn't really think straight and definitely couldn't talk very well, but I rode and rode until I tracked her down. By the time I found her I was barely coherent.

Of course she was hurt and angry that I had been gone for so long, but upon seeing my festering leg she immediately sprang into action. She quickly readied the bike trailer for travel, hooked it up and then propped me up on some pillows inside it. In a flash we were underway and, although I was heavy and it was a lot of work for her, she pedaled furiously to the emergency room. It was far away so it took her a while to get there, but she chugged along without stopping. Once there, she took me to the door, hugged me, and said, "Good luck baby, I'll see you soon." With that, I turned and went inside.

My knife was confiscated immediately upon my arrival. Next came all of the paperwork. Despair. Hurt. Fear. Loneliness. All of these feelings and more welled up inside me as I completed the questionnaire in its sparse, barren, entirety.

Phone number: none
Address: none
Next of kin: none
Emergency phone number: none
Employer: none
Insurance provider: none
Method of payment: none

And so on, and so on. By the time I had finished filling out and signing all of the authorizations, waivers and disclaimers, I almost felt like dying was the better option. Of course I already knew all of these things to be true, but seeing them laid out before me on paper was gut wrenching. There it was, for all the world to see: I had nothing and I had no one.

Because I didn't have an ID, I assumed that the hospital would be no different than every other agency in town and would deny me service. Even if they did decide to help me, I figured I would be of very low priority. I mentally prepared myself to spend the night in the waiting room.

The nurse in charge took one look at my leg and immediately called upstairs. Mind you, the Fresno ER is a combat medic's dream. They get to practice on gunshots, stab wounds and blunt force traumas all night, every night. When I was whisked to the front of the line, I knew that it was serious. I wasn't there ten minutes when I was greeted by a team of two doctors and four nurses. They took me to a private room on an upper floor and the looks on their faces were grave.

The doctor informed me that I had MRSA and that I might not have made it there soon enough. He told me there was a chance that they might have to take my leg. I took the news quietly, even stoically, but when they left the room I sobbed myself to sleep. To say that I was at a low point in my life is an understatement. I was incredibly lonely and hurting tremendously and there was nobody to blame but myself. The rest of the night was a blur. I do remember being awoken by a nurse and a large orderly as they expressed the vile substance from my leg. It felt like they were pushing battery acid out through the swollen wound. The pain was absolutely vehement.

I can't tell you whether I was there for hours or days, but eventually I was given a pair of crutches and was released in the middle of the night. I was incredibly worried about having to trek back through the hood at that hour on crutches, too weak to fight back. If I ever felt like a victim, it was at that moment. Fortunately, I didn't find any more trouble that evening and I was able to hobble back to a safe place where I could rest and heal accordingly.

Sometimes, miracles have no explanation.

At that point, I was really beginning to feel like I wasn't supposed to have a left leg. Years before, I had completely shredded my ACL, MCL and meniscus, which required surgery to repair it. Then, I nearly lost the same leg to MRSA. The infection had almost healed completely when I got bit by a large black widow spider just below the previous infection site. It hurt, of course, and swelled up instantly, but after my last ailment I wasn't very concerned. Having survived MRSA, I figured this was pretty minor. I mean, they're super creepy and sinister looking, but it's only a spider, right?

I assumed that it wouldn't be long before the pain would go away and the swelling would subside. This was not the case. The swelling didn't get much worse, but the redness spread up my leg and felt like a wave of white hot fire. I could literally feel this wave of fire start in my leg and slowly spread through my entire body. More fever and chills. I was probably going into shock for all I knew. I decided against returning to the emergency room because I felt silly for requesting services for a simple spider bite.

Of course I had been up to my usual antics, which meant no sleep, no food and no water. Looking back, I'm surprised that my body was able to combat the effects of the venom considering all of these extenuating circumstances. I guzzled as much water as I could stand and tucked inside to hide. With my legs elevated, I covered myself with an old blanket while I slept.

I don't know how long I was there, but when I awoke I knew that I would be ok. Although I still felt like my skin was burning off, my head felt clearer. Physically speaking, my recovery time was relatively quick, however it was quite a while before I stopped assuming that every little rustle and every faint little tickle or itch was another black widow spider.

Piranhas

California is a world of contradictions. On one hand, it has the best of everything. The weather is nice and the lifestyle is glamorous. A good portion of the residents are beautiful and their possessions are as well. The state itself is known as the "Land Of Dreams" and having the pinnacle of nearly every profession represented there seems to lend truth to this claim. Also, let's not forget that "California Style" is a legendary expression which is emulated worldwide.

As the pendulum swings, you notice that California also has the worst of everything. It boasts one of the worst gang problems in America, which ultimately leads to it having one of the toughest prison systems in the world. Horrendously awful statistics for homicides, drug abuse, divorce rates, unemployment and homelessness also add to its misfortune.

Fresno holds true, in many ways, to these same patterns. Located in the Central Valley, it is surrounded by farmland and agricultural industry. Hardworking people scratch out for a meager existence. Here, pride is found in the fight, not in the victory. This tough work ethic aids in the success of many, but not all. Battered by economic hardship and racial tension, a lot of people lose hope.

In the poorer neighborhoods, death and suffering are the rule rather than the exception. Yet, even in the midst of all of this, there are shining examples of kindness and humanity. Somebody's laptop, phone, purse or wallet might be stolen without batting an eyelash, yet food is almost always shared with the hungry, sometimes even by those who are hungry themselves. The same single mothers who are forced to sell their bodies to subsist, sometimes get food or formula gifted to them in a random fashion.

These contradictions boggled me at first. I just couldn't see the patterns. Nothing fit cleanly into my understanding of things. As more time passed, I began to see these same inconsistencies within myself. My actions did not always mesh with my intentions. Sometimes my integrity was breached and my moral code bent in the name of survival. I was becoming who I wasn't. Or maybe that's who I was? All of my former thoughts and perceptions were tainted horribly by the things that I had seen and done.

It seemed that a lot of times, I became who I was most afraid of. This happens to us all, to a certain degree, but in extenuating circumstances the effects are amplified. For instance, if you are afraid of a gun-carrying robber, a lot of times you end up thinking like a gun-carrying robber to avoid becoming the victim of a gun-carrying robber. At that point it becomes counterproductive; you end up being no different than the person you are fighting against. There was, however, a silver lining. I found some of my greatest truths and most powerful moments of peace during this time. They were rare, for the jumble of clatter in my mind wouldn't normally allow them, but I did find them.

Almost without fail, I would choose alleys for moving from place to place. I found it better to stay out of the public eye and wander the byways undetected. At least it felt better. Unbeknownst to most, there's a whole different world beneath the glossy veneer of the beautiful building facades. For most, if not carefully coiffed, painted and presented, it's not seen. My paths took me through the heart of what was real, not what was presented. Through the neglected parts. Through the sagging, dirty, wretched parts. Only mere feet from what was supposed to be seen, were the heaps of garbage and foulness, structures crumbled in ruin and teemed with vermin.

Some of these buildings were attractive from front to back, through and through, well cared for and maintained. Pride was obviously taken in every aspect of their operation and upkeep. These were the rare exceptions. My world, on the fringes, was not so brightly painted. It was dull brick and cinder block. It was dust and soot and refuse. It was random discord and ugliness. That is precisely what made the few so beautiful. Their rarity heralding their attributes. The contrast lending to their allure. Their beauty only then appreciated.

I remember certain days when so many things would go wrong that it was almost funny. Literally. When each of my ill-fated steps only moved me from one calamity to the next, when the black cloud of my ill-fortune would choke me with one bad turn after another. I would watch everyday people drive by in their cars and notice how foreign they looked in their benign normalcy. I would laugh and laugh and laugh. It was ridiculous to me that I had allowed myself to be there. Yet, there I was, day after day.

One of the residents of our camp, who I simply referred to as Cuba, offered a prime example of this absurdness. I had known him off and on for years. He had approached me some time back about joining him for hit contracts, which I had politely declined. Most of the time he kept to himself; I don't think he cared much for being around people. He appeared to be a very tortured soul. Every once in a while, he would lose his grip on reality and would become insanely violent.

At the time, my preference in weapons were a pair of throwing tomahawks which I had constructed using old axe heads. They were ground down into an exaggerated, blade-heavy form, reminiscent of the Old Saxon war axes. I added to it a thick-walled metal pipe, which I cut off at the appropriate length to compliment my throwing technique. This wasn't a "lobber", like you see demonstrated at logging shows, nor was it manufactured for a slow swooping flight. These I had made short, heavy and blade forward. They were to be thrown hard and fast. Because of their short axis and great balance, they had a fast flip. They ran true and hit very hard. I practiced with these from every position and every angle. I dialed in at fifteen to twenty feet, common pistol range in those parts, and I was very fast on the draw. I never missed.

Cuba had been running amuck through the camp and was screaming incoherently. He was making threatening advances towards each of us and seemed particularly fixated on me. I slowly walked out of camp and into the large, windswept, clearing on the outskirts. Overshadowed by the enormous feed silos, and in plain sight of their crews, I knew things were going to get ridiculous when he started following me out.

He was still screaming at me. Now, with room to work, I screamed back. He started running across the two hundred yard gap between us, waving his spear and brandishing his long knife. I reached for my axes, which I always carried in my belt, and took them in each hand. When he got within fifty feet of me, I stopped walking, turned and sprinted directly towards him, axes at the ready. In a flash, I had reached the perfect point for release. It echoed what I had done a thousand times before in practice. I timed the raise of my axe so that I would release the throw with my next footfall. He was so close it would be impossible for me to miss. I planned to bury the first one in his chest and finish him with the second one.

Oblivious, he came straight in. We were in the middle of the huge clearing. It was early afternoon and the workers had lined the silos to watch the combat. As I started to release, in the split second of its entirety, I couldn't. Instead, I side-stepped at an angle just out of spear range. He was tired from the run and I could have easily dispatched him, but I didn't. In lieu, I danced around and taunted him while clanging my axes together in true Viking fashion. I asked myself many times afterwards, *Had those workers not been watching, would I have done it? Would I have ended that man's life? Should I have?*

He wasn't a decent person, I knew that much for sure. I had spoken with someone who had personally witnessed Cuba finishing somebody off with a straight razor, right along those very tracks. Maybe if he had backed me into a corner I would have done it, but not in this manner. I had the clear advantage. I chose not to kill him and I still survived. That alone testifies that it would have been wrong, that I made the right choice, even if it meant looking over my shoulder the rest of my time there.

It was all so surreal in its absurdity. Think about it. Two homeless guys, clad only in shorts, running at each other pell-mell, intent on a clash of weapons in the middle of a sun-scorched, open field. It was like something out of the movie *Gladiator*. I would often find myself in these types of situations. They defied logic, and sometimes were so ridiculous that it was almost funny. Yet, it wasn't funny at all. It was life or death. Day after day. I learned to expect that anything could happen, no matter how ludicrous. My parameters of perception broadened greatly because of this. It's amazing what we can see, hear, smell and sense when not constrained by the specifications of logic or rational thought.

As much as a lot of my life on the streets resembled a high-action flick or video game, it was not its entirety. It wasn't always filled with a whirling subterfuge of treachery and explosive violence. Oftentimes, I would drift away, transfixed by the beauty of a sunrise or the sound of a bird singing or the feel of the sun on my skin. What a beautiful paradox.

I still don't understand why then, only then, in that life, did I truly experience these things for the first time. When I had nothing. Dazzling in its simplicity, breathtakingly beautiful, for what it was. Just what it was. Not what it meant, or why it was, or who else felt it or who didn't. Just a beautiful gift. In those rare moments, when my mind was quiet enough to receive them, I was able to accept these priceless gifts as just that. I feel very fortunate to have been blessed in this manner during some of my most trying times.

Contradictions abound in seemingly every aspect of life, but especially when you are living on the streets. Just as close acquaintances can become a threat or a liability, sometimes the converse is actually true. On a few occasions, I was able to turn a threat of mine into an asset. Such was the case with the small packs of wild dogs that roamed the wasteland around our camp. A lot of them were mistreated and abandoned and some of them were born feral. I came to know one of them, a large female named Princess.

She resembled a hyena, both in her markings and in her traits. She was quite fearsome. When we first moved into camp, I would often surprise her in our tent or food storage area. Initially, my intentions were to kill her. She scared me. I would frequently turn suddenly in the dark, only to find that she had been stalking me. She would lie in ambush, coiled to pounce at just the right moment. As the days stretched into weeks, and the weeks into months, we grew amicable with each other's company.

As I learned more about her, a grudging respect formed within me. This propagated into something of a kinship as the grueling hardship stretched on and on. Much like me, she could rely on no one. Kindness was a stranger who rarely visited. Having been abused by her former owner, and then abandoned, she was forced into survival. Forgotten and alone, she was without comfort and joy. She took what she needed. She was fierce, fast, cunning and strong.

Over time, familiarity grew between us and it came to be that I would share my food with her. Even when given, she would seize it and withdraw to the shadows, as if she had claimed it by force. She never came to beg for food and she never waited for me to feed her. But if she were there, and I happened to be eating, I would share. It gave me a small measure of comfort to do this. I hope that it eased her misery a bit as well.

I was never able to pet her, but then again, I never really tried. Our relationship was not that. Ours was one of rival predators who tolerated each other, only because it would be too risky to try to eliminate each other. Even after we had known each other for quite a while, even after she had warmed to my presence in the area, even after she would sometimes wag her tail when she saw me, I would still sometimes turn to see her stalking me. Every time I would ride my bike from camp after dark, she would spring from the blackness and try to tear me off, an inky whirlwind of gnashing teeth and corded muscle.

But in the manner of most things out here, there was a contradiction to this. A paradox that made this nemesis of mine, an ally. Because I knew of this creature, and I knew of her ways, it gave me an edge. There were many times when people came to camp after dark, looking to do me harm. Time and again, she would drive intruders away, savaging their limbs during their flight. She didn't do this out of allegiance to me, but out of instinct born from hardship. She did this to survive. In turn, it helped me to survive.

You see, when you swim with piranhas, that's all you have to worry about. Not crocs. Not snakes. Not boars. Not jaguars. Only piranhas. As long as I didn't show any weakness or aggression towards her, she would recognize my place there. Those who were not recognized had a cruel surprise waiting for them in the dark.

Marshall Law

As things became bleaker, and the air in the city became more hopeless, the very nature of our enclaves changed. What were once harmless little communities tucked out of view from the mainstream world, had now grown into bustling networks of grimy settlements. More and more of the lawless types were using our areas as waypoints and rest stops. They would slink through and negotiate items for a meal, a change of clothes, a place to rest or a weapon. Although I did not endorse or participate in a lot of illegal activities, I did live in a manner that was, at best, marginal. We all did.

Harlots now visibly plied their trade in our camp. Drugs were openly bought, sold, traded and used. Violence was displayed regularly. A thriving trade of stolen goods was at every camp, ours being no exception, with neighbors often robbing neighbors and selling it to another neighbor. It had all gone horribly wrong. We had established our camp to be a springboard of sorts, a safe place from which we could attempt to claw our way back to a semblance of regular life. It had become anything but that.

As the camp grew, it meant that there were more people competing for the same resources. This led to our impact on the area becoming much greater and areas becoming "blown out", or rendered unusable. As we were forced to expand, we became more visible. Now, we weren't just an occasional eyesore to be ignored and hurried by, we were a threat. Instead of the authorities viewing us with a cool, detached indifference, we were now a recognized problem. The problem wasn't that we were homeless and without food or water, but that we were now part of mainstream society. The residents could see us now and that made people uncomfortable.

The homeless quickly became synonymous with crime and all that was unwanted in a society. If these labels didn't stick in the beginning, they sure did in the end. I suppose this happens everywhere, human nature corrupting and tainting something that was supposed to be good and making it vile. As our little community became a spot on the map of the "who's who of Fresno criminal activity", things got worse. Our outings and forays extended out into a wider circle, with more and more of the city becoming exposed to our onslaught. As more of us traveled to and from this epicenter, the heat came back with us. Formerly left alone, we were now raided regularly.

Police patrols, resembling military units, now patrolled the low income neighborhoods aggressively. If you were out after dark, you were usually arrested. At the very least, you were detained for a bit and roughed up. The tank and the city's SWAT team made raid after raid within sight of our encampment, resplendent with loud explosions given off by the breaching charges and the occasional gunshots, always with the barking and snarling of their ferocious German shepherds who accompanied them.

In our world, the police were considered the enemy. Not only because of our criminal activity, but because of our social standing. The police here were different than the police that I'd known in other cities. They were just like the people that I was dealing with in the underworld on a daily basis, only in a different uniform. A few were decent, but the majority of them treated us horribly. We didn't vote. We didn't pay taxes. We didn't have jobs. We didn't look or act like everybody else. We were all the same to them. If anyone bothered to call for help, they never came. We weren't worthy of help.

It didn't matter that some of us were just regular citizens who had lost homes when unemployment shot up and the housing market crashed, that some were mentally ill and were simply unable to get the care they needed, that some were drug addicts so ravaged by their disease that they saw no other way out, that some were veterans returning home from war with such severe PTSD that they were incapable of functioning normally, that some were felons fresh out of prison with nothing of their former life left to go back to and that some were victims of violent crimes who were so broken that they were unable to return to their normal lives. None of this mattered.

Once, as I walked down a sidewalk in the Tower District, I was accosted by a policeman. After running my name, searching me and firing off the usual questions, he told me that I had to leave the area. "Your kind doesn't belong here." he said, "If I ever see you around here again, you'll be sorry." I told him that I lived in the area and that I didn't know anywhere else. He responded by saying, "Not anymore you don't. As far as I'm concerned, you're a thief and a druggie and I'm going to treat you as such." His words cut through me like a knife. I felt that it was wrong of him to say these things to me, but then again, he was right. I *was* a thief and a druggie.

I didn't want to be the enemy. I didn't want to be the "bad guy" or the "problem". I just was. We all were. At that point, it felt as if battle lines had been drawn. Once in motion, both sides were swept along by the momentum, unwitting and sometimes unwilling participants in the struggle. So very different, yet each the same in our will to survive, staunchly defending our way of life and our right to life.

Even before the bottom fell out, the authorities seemed to be against me. When I still had my apartment in the Tower District, and work became intermittent, I opened up an informal bike shop in my garage. I acquired various parts from garage sales and trash bins and was able to make functioning bicycles from them. I would also make repairs and find parts for people. A lot of low income folks utilized bikes for their primary transportation and I prided myself on keeping the neighborhood rolling.

When making repairs, I would only ask for food, a few dollars, a pack of cigarettes or a beer as payment. Nobody was refused, regardless of their inability to pay. This went on for quite a few months. Everybody was happy. My customers were staying mobile and their contributions were helpful to me. It wasn't long before the police started hassling me on a regular basis. They told me that they had heard I was running a "chop shop" for bicycles. I encouraged them to hurry up and whip out their notebooks so they could start recording serial numbers; I told them that I was in the business of building bikes, not taking them apart. It was 100+

degrees in my garage so they took a quick glance and left.

After this incident they would often appear, always with something to say, but I never had any reason for them to find trouble. Finally, they came and shut me down. Apparently, I wasn't allowed to fix bicycles without a business license. According to them, the owners of the local bike shops had complained. They were only enforcing the law.... Yeah. Okay. I still wonder why they chose to focus so much of their time on a guy who may, or may not, have been violating a simple business infraction. Meanwhile, there were people getting shot in the streets daily. It certainly didn't make any sense to me. Tired of being hassled, I finally complied.

I often wondered what happened to everyone I knew. I would roll through familiar neighborhoods where I used to know everyone and not recognize a single face. Neighborhood after neighborhood, the same story. It was disconcerting. When I got to County, I found out why. I recognized just about everybody in there. Life on the streets was starting to catch up with everyone. Some had worse outcomes than others.

One day I heard that a homeless man had been gunned down in the Tower District at the community gardens. At first, many thought it was me. I matched the victim's description perfectly: shaved head, chinstrap beard, wearing only a pair of baggy, drab olive shorts with a large knife tucked into his belt. Encircled by officers, he was gunned down when he refused to immediately comply. That's what things were coming to.

I recognized a lot of the formations that the police were using from my military days. Scores of two and three-man teams moved throughout the night, raiding and striking. Of course this was never in the news. They moved like they had a purpose and appeared very confident. Some thought they were from the Cartel, but I had to agree with the school of thought that they were instead Fed hit teams.

They were very skilled. I gave them the slip quite a few times but they employed some pretty advanced tactics so it wasn't easy to do so. They would often utilize a trail and flankers, sometimes even two trails. That second rascal was almost the end of me once, but that's a story probably not to be told. Interestingly enough, they seemed to communicate and coordinate very well.

Once, instead of regressing after I had given a team the slip, I followed them and posted up at a hidden overlook. To my amazement, three other teams converged on their location, and what looked like a senior officer got to the front and appeared to be lecturing them. It was almost like the AAR's, or after action reviews, that we had in my old military recon unit after an engagement. This did not bode well with me. All of a sudden, the whole game changed. The entire area felt like a DMZ, or demilitarized zone under martial law.

The helicopters circled incessantly. Every sight and sound resembled that of a nation under occupation. As trying as it was for us, strangely, I found myself struggling to blame the police for this scourge. I understood full and well where we stood. I had once been a family man. A homeowner. A taxpayer. A citizen. I can only guess their opinions of us. We were a danger, a threat to their way of life. Hell, we weren't even people any more, but rather a problem to be done away with. A nameless, faceless blemish. An eyesore. How much better things would be if we would just disappear. Please believe me when I tell you that I wanted that too, I just had nowhere to go.

For whatever reason, nobody likes to speak of these things, this undercurrent of our nation. What we cannot deny, is that there are people out there, just like you and me, who lurk on the fringes of our lives. People who are devastated. Ruined. Hopeless. Although our everyday choices ultimately lead to these ends, we don't choose to be broken and without hope. Yet, it happens to a frightening number of us. Homeless camps aren't being bulldozed simply because they are criminal in nature. These same crimes and problems are present everywhere, intricately woven and interlaced through mainstream life. These camps are being bulldozed because nobody wants to see the symptoms of a greater problem.

By the time I arrived at County for an extended period of time, the zone was so blown out that it was probably just as well. Everything had changed. The logistics and day to day routines (or lack of) had changed. The socio-political climate had changed. *I had changed.* As things became harder and harder, simple joy became unattainable. I was so tired. Tired of trying. Tired of failing. Tired of having to work so damn hard for things as simple as a bite to eat or something to drink.

Being forced to scatter from camp meant that we were thrust into unfamiliar grounds. This made things exponentially more dangerous because we were unaccustomed to the patterns and workings of the new neighborhoods. It also meant that you had to put in much more time and effort for much less return. Yes, everything had changed. This wasn't fun anymore.

Cars

Fresno County Jail was like nothing I had ever seen. Overcrowding was such an issue that for years I committed crimes with relative impunity. The soaring crime rate and the economic hardship of the county rendered the legal system next to useless. Federal money seemed to be about the only thing that kept the doors from swinging open and letting all of us back out onto the streets. As it was, it was quite a while before I ever had to serve any time for my offenses.

When I finally did serve time, even after being arrested for several felonies, I was out the very next morning. It didn't seem to matter that I had a record with violent felonies in another state. As far as the California Department of Corrections (DOC) was concerned, I was a squeaky clean square. No strikes, no prison priors, no parole or probation holds. Nothing. I was brand new.

As soon as I was released, I was given a court date. I never showed up. I didn't have money to eat, let alone pay court fees. It went on like this for over a year. I must have been arrested and released about eleven times on the same warrant, many times accruing a new drug, weapon or resisting charge for whatever I had on me or how I was acting at the time.

Eventually, I was finally sent "upstairs" and my introduction to the California Correctional System began. I had previously served three years in a maximum security prison up in Alaska, but the California system made that stint feel like I had been away at summer camp. When asked if I had any gang ties, I replied "No." When asked if I had beef with anybody, I again replied "No." They photographed and catalogued my tattoos, fingerprinted me, searched me, gave me a wristband and sent me to pick up my county issue before heading up.

At this facility, county issue consisted of three red jumpsuits, three pairs of boxers, three pairs of socks, three towels (which were usually all pink from being laundered with the jumpsuits), a toothbrush, a comb, a rule booklet and one pair of flip flops. "Wood," they said, "5th floor." As it turned out I was headed for an active gang pod. "Wood" was a name used to distinguish white convicts, or active criminals able enough to survive in general population.

As soon as you arrive in your pod, you are greeted by a rep from your "car", or racial group. If you are unknown, someone from your car will immediately check your papers. The white car typically holds the highest standards as to who is allowed to reside in the pod. Persons who have committed crimes of a sexual nature or any crimes against children are not allowed. Rats, or snitches, are not allowed either. If they weren't beaten or cut on the spot, at the very least, they were denied residence. This was done by simply ringing the buzzer to alert the guard. Without so much as a word, they would come and take them away. Most who fell under this category immediately opted for PC, or protective custody, and didn't even try to survive in general population.

Molesters, otherwise known as Chesters, are considered the bottom of the food chain, the lowest scum of all scum. You will never find one in general population. They are either in PC, the infirmary or the morgue. Not surprising, in street etiquette, it's a perpetual "green light" to take down Chesters. Inside or out. This is a policy that I fully support.

Although I wasn't gang affiliated, it was important to me that I remain in general population, even if it meant that I was in more danger. It would be abhorrent to me to be perceived as falling into either of the categories that required PC.

I'm not a racist. I'm not a bigot. I could give a damn what somebody's ethnic background is. None of this matters. In the California DOC, I was in the white car. Period. I was a Fresno Wood. A free, unaffiliated, Anglo from Fresno County, down to stand up for mine and capable of fighting if necessary. If another white was in the mix, I was to jump in and stand shoulder to shoulder with him. If he was wrong in the issue, then he was to be punished by us, white men in a white cell.

It took me a very long time to see this for what it was. I didn't like any of it. I mistakenly thought that hatred and ignorance were at play. It's not that. These structures have been in place in the California Correctional System for over forty years. What surprised me was that these crazy structures actually circumvented much more trouble than it stirred up. Having each person responsible not only for themselves, but for their peers, negated hundreds of petty squabbles every single day.

If one person in the pod started swinging, everybody did. Within minutes, it would spread from pod to pod and floor to floor. This meant that the goon squads would come in. They were very liberal with their use of non-lethal force. CS shots from paintball guns, bean bag and block projectiles, stun guns and batons were all applied by the armored troops in an aggressive manner in order to regain control. We would be locked down and any small comforts that we had been privy to would screech to a halt during isolation.

Now don't be mistaken, many altercations still take place inside. Inmate on inmate violence is prevalent within each organization. Disputes are settled and authority is asserted on a cell by cell basis. While only involved in a handful of situations of my own, I witnessed a significant amount of altercations firsthand. Out of respect for the inmate code, those details will not be discussed by me. I'm only here to tell my tale, not theirs.

What I will say, is that every couple of days the stewards would mop up buckets of blood from the segregation cells. Inmates, some already crazy, would be driven over the edge by the isolation. A lot of them would use the tiny razor blades from our shaving razors. Some would use pencils (the ones issued a mere three inches long), and others would beat their heads against the doors or walls until they split open. It's hard to say if they really wanted to die. Perhaps they were just bored and thought the infirmary would be a nice change of scenery.

The racial boundaries that are in place in the California system are extensive. I didn't like to play along, but when it came down to it being a matter of survival, I eventually learned to march to the prescribed tune. There was, however, a steep learning curve for me. My fierce independence and non-allegiance meant that I bowed to no one. A few respected my values, and acknowledged my warrior spirit on occasion, but as a whole, they assumed I was stupid for initially bucking the system. It sickened me that I had to swallow my principles in order to survive. Nobody else seemed to mind, everything had been set in stone for quite some time. For those who grew up in the area, the rules were very clear. In my case, they were quite foreign.

There was a black TV and a Bulldog TV. A black dip bar and a Bulldog dip bar. A black pull-up bar and a Bulldog pull-up bar. The blacks had certain tables and the Bulldogs had certain tables. We had certain tables. We were to sit at our tables and they were to sit at theirs. The black pull-up bars and dip bars were completely off limits to us, but the Bulldog's could be used if not already in use. Accruing gambling debts or drug debts with any other races was a big no-no. Too many things could go wrong with putting money on the books and a discrepancy could cause things to kick off.

There were rules for everything, even for the order in which you lined up for chow. The Bulldogs always went first because they had the most numbers, next were the whites and last were the blacks because they were "too cool to care". Of course no one initially explained any of this to me, I had to learn by simple observation and trial and error.

The food inside was dismal. There was never enough to satisfy the ravenous hunger that I brought in with me. I found myself marking time by each upcoming meal. How many minutes until it got to the floor? Which pod would be served first? What would it be? It seems ridiculous to have an obsession with such meager fare, but it was literally the only thing that I had to look forward to. It was always bland and soggy and there was never enough. Apparently, some dietitian figured that we only needed 1000 calories a day to survive. Day after day, I cursed the very existence of this professional punisher. My body was literally in starvation mode when I arrived and that didn't change much as time wore on.

Most of the guys inside were career criminals. These "hard cases" received assistance from the outside. Their mommies would send them money. Or their wives. Or their whores. Big, tough, gangsters crying on the phone, begging for money. Had to have their commissary. Had to have their comfort items. I really felt nothing but contempt for this aspect of the thug life. Leaving behind everyone who depended on them and then expecting those same people to supply snacks and pay off their gambling debts. What a bunch of sissies. *Suffer like a man,* I would think.

Even still, I would always feel alone on commissary days. Everyone else was happy and smiling, an exuberant air permeated the entire pod. It was hard to ignore. I didn't have anybody to help ease my suffering and shower me with love and gifts. No one even knew I was inside. When I lost my backpack, I lost all of my contacts. I tried to tell myself, *It's only right, you got yourself into this mess, you have to get yourself out of this mess.* Still, it didn't make things any easier.

Although food was the only thing that I had to look forward to each day, it also created quite a problem for me. My actions, regarding how I obtained my food, were not met with approval by the rest of my car. If someone left food on their tray, I would intercept them on the way to the trash. White. Brown. Black. I didn't care. My hunger was insatiable. This definitely raised eyebrows. Initially, others pretended not to see this flagrant breach of etiquette. Whites are not supposed to eat any unsealed or unwrapped food from a black. Apparently, this rule originated because the blacks don't screen their car as stringently, they prefer having larger numbers over a "cleaner" car. This doesn't sit well with the whites who have the opposite viewpoint.

I was finally approached by the white rep and asked to stop. I was told that it wasn't good for the younger whites to see my behavior; they were young and impressionable and wouldn't understand how things were supposed to be done. I replied with a stoic expression, "You're right, a white boy should feed me." There were whites in there with hundreds of dollars in extra food each week, yet I wasn't invited to any of their spreads or snack parties because I didn't have commissary. They never accepted me from the start because I didn't bow down to them. But please believe, if they were ever in trouble, they'd be my best friend, hiding right behind me. It was a very one-sided relationship.

The pods were usually organized as such: about 30 Bulldogs, 15-20 blacks and about 10 whites (if we were lucky). Because of these numbers, things got very political. I, on the other hand, preferred a zero tolerance policy. If I were disrespected in the slightest, I was ready to throw down. In fact, I always used to say that County was the safest place in Fresno because there weren't any guns. I could hold my own against a couple dozen Mexicans throwing blows, but one punk with a gun could end my life in an instant.

One day a Bulldog, who had a life sentence, demanded that I do something for him. I told him, "No. Nobody tells me to do anything." We exchanged hard looks and were about to brawl. The white rep and his buddy immediately called me over to talk. Being new to the system, I had no idea what was going on. The three of us entered his cell and he proceeded to yell at me. In not so nice of words, I told him to shut up. He threw a fast six piece combo at my face, catching me unaware. Instead of falling, like he expected, I dipped him hard and balled him up next to the steel bunks.

As I was immobilizing him and freeing up my arm to re-organize his face, I heard his buddy say, "That's the rep, you can't do that. I should stab you right now." I was unsure as to what I was supposed to do, so I halted and stepped back. His buddy punched me, broke his hand on my face, and then proceeded to lecture me on how wrong I was to start beef with the Bulldogs. It was very confusing. I assumed that the white car was simply scared of the Bulldog's numbers so they sacrificed one of their own to show that the "matter was handled".

I soon realized, that even though I had a car, I was really all alone. No one had my back. In fact, my "own people" were the only ones who ever put their hands on me while I was inside. This actually isn't uncommon. Those who are closest to you can see the chinks in your armor, they know your weaknesses and know how to exploit them. If the whites had a stronger car, I can only assume that I would have been beaten to death in a white cell. I have Filipina children. My most recent companion, Nashelle, is mulatto. I ran in a predominately Hispanic area. I knew a lot of the Bulldogs in the pod from out on the bricks and I conversed with them. I ate a lot of food that the blacks had touched. I basically did as I wished.

Fortunately, our car was very light in numbers so they needed my help to keep us from getting steamrolled if things popped off. From then on, I really kept to myself. I was still a valued member of the car, but I could no longer tolerate any of the members. As I endlessly circled the pod, day after day, countless scenarios played out in my head about the vengeance that I was going to exact on them.

It worked out well that I was accustomed to spending the majority of my time alone, because jail is a very, very, lonely place. Even more so if no one even knows you are there. Minutes seemed to stretch into eternity with nothing but the same mundane walls to stare at. It didn't help that there was very little to do inside. Programs, or other resources, were nonexistent. It was punishment. Plain and simple. We did not leave the pod except for an hour, once a week, to the cage up on the roof. When I scaled the chain link walls of the cage I could almost see my camp. It was torture, but I couldn't fight the compulsion not to do so.

If I had a solid group of friends inside, as many others did, things would have been much easier in some respects. Coasting through my sentence, I would have been safe and well fed. Time would have flown by with conversation and wild jailhouse antics. I watched others around me almost giddy when another "homie" arrived. Reunion after reunion, it seemed that most of them got out just long enough to make a couple of new stories to tell in the pod. So inept at a regular existence, they actually preferred things to be structured and regimented so that they never had to make any decisions.

This slowly happens to all of us if we let it. It's called institutionalization. Places like County encourage exactly that. It's a finishing school for criminals, a passage in your resume. Techniques are shared, contacts made, plots schemed and information traded. It's underworld networking at its finest. All day. Every day. The only "good life" that is spoken of refers to getting high, screwing whores and messing people up.

I chose to focus elsewhere. Nobody can be immune to this so one must make a great effort to avoid it. My outlaw mentality went way back, so it wasn't easy, but I wanted to be a slave no longer. I started letting my thoughts examine philosophical principles that I had been reading. This led to a lot of questions about things, questions about myself. Introspection is a fearsome thing when you're already at an extreme low, but I really had nothing more to lose.

I finally came to accept the fact that my destiny relied solely in my hands. Once I discovered this, I was no longer trapped. Courses of action that I didn't agree with, or principles that I stood for, didn't have to be brushed aside out of obligation or loyalty. In short, because I had no one, I was free. Not free in the literal sense of course, but free to be me. Sure there was risk, but it was worth it to me. Coming to terms with this was part of the spark that culminated in me changing my life. It didn't happen overnight, and it definitely didn't come easy, but it eventually happened.

My first week or so inside, I slept as much as possible. Waking only for meals, I was able to "easy time" it. I had been running hard. Once my body caught up, I was sleeping less and less. With nothing to occupy my thoughts except sorrow and regrets, it was hard not to lose my mind. Like a shark in a tank, I circled the pod endlessly. I would walk a lap as slowly as possible and do a set of push-ups or dips. I did this all day and most of the night. Every day. Every night.

As I walked, I would try to remember every detail of Jujitsu sequences that I had learned. Subtleties and nuances of grappling and striking. A lot of the things that I had learned while training had fallen into disuse. It was almost a form of meditation, except that I was focusing on memories and trying to relive the feel of my body carrying out the correct mechanics of the movements.

It was frustrating how slowly my progress was at first. I had to will my mind to focus on what I chose. Memories were distant. My mind cloudy. My thoughts not used to being consciously shaped or formed. This is exactly how I began to regain control of myself. This methodology encompassed all of it, my mind, body and spirit. And it came, slowly albeit, but it came. While I walked, I forced my mind to a specific thought or memory. Once this became clear, I forced every detail to come into sharp focus and I would then replay them in sequence. In the correct manner. In the correct order.

When I would do my push-ups or dips with each lap, I would concentrate not only on the perfect execution of repetition, but on feeling the recruitment and firing of each specific muscle group, down to the fibers. This helped repair my mind-muscle link. It all sounds very odd, but it was imperative. After being so instinctive and reflexive for so long, it was crucial that I start regaining some control. Animals rely on instinct, humans rely on controlled choices.

At first, these exercises weren't a conscious decision. I was simply narrowing my cognitive focus to a specific thing in order to help pass the time. The trick, however, was to remain completely aware of my surroundings in order to continue processing everything. The difference was, now, I was letting my subconscious, which I trust, process what was actually a threat and what wasn't.

How interesting it was, that in order to regain control of everything, I had to surrender control at the same time. Instead of watching and listening to every minute detail, I let my body do that, while my mind did my bidding. I really feel that this was an important step towards the change in me that was necessary. I refused to go on any longer in an unrestrained or impulsive manner, at the mercy of my own thoughts. I could choose them, and not only that, I could shape them. All said, I must have walked hundreds of miles in there.

While learning to shape my thoughts, I did face a very tough obstacle. After years of meth use and the emotional wasteland that comes with it, my feelings were starting to come back. I suppose eating and sleeping play a large role in brain chemistry as well. I could *feel* again. I was all over the place. Up. Down. Everywhere in-between. It was fairly hard to deal with at first, but my new focusing techniques helped a lot. I realized that even if I weren't able to control my feelings, I could most definitely control my thoughts. This kept me from being completely irrational in my actions.

There are three things that are deferred to at County and any place like it: money, power and savagery. Like on the outside, money controls everything. Those who had it, made the rules for everybody else and did as they wanted. This was a problem for me. If the rules weren't going to be followed by all, then I wasn't going to follow them either.

The second two go hand-in-hand. One must be ready at all times to either kill or die for who he is and what he stands for, no matter what that is. The details are really of no consequence, it is the raw elemental fact that holds. Inside and outside (on the streets) really parallel each other regarding this matter. People, especially inmates, seem to gravitate towards strength. They also fear it. Power is usually not held for long and the balance quickly shifts. If you are feared, you are in just as much danger as if you are weak. If you falter for a second, they will put you to the ground. You're done.

I've seen some pretty dangerous men swaggering around the pod, in complete control. The next day, these same men were being pushed from their pod in a wheelchair, faces unrecognizable. One of them, I've got to hand it to him, kept going back to his pod each time he was released from the infirmary. Refusing to enter PC, he realized that all he had left was to show heart. He was repeatedly beaten, again and again. Soon after, the guy who was responsible for these beatings was released. While serving out my sentence, I heard that he was gunned down on Belmont and Yosemite. Ah, the wages of sin. Everything carries consequence. If you're in that game, and you have an angle on somebody, you'd better use it. The tables always turn, and at some point, they'll have the angle on you.

With that said, I do believe that the universe, or divinity, or whatever regulates such things, does show some sentiment. On many occasions, predominantly for the health of my own psyche, I have shown mercy to those deserving retribution. I spared them when I knew that it was dangerous to do so. This has shown itself to grow and multiply in beauty with every minute that has passed since then.

I specifically remember standing over a foe that had publicly threatened my life. His room was dark as he slept in the presumed safety of his home. His pit bulls were silenced, his locks negated. Every advantage was mine. As I held the three foot metal pipe over my head, poised to end this danger, I almost cried when I heard the words ringing in my head, *This is what he would do. Are you no better than him?* Shaking with the tension of the moment, I lowered the pipe. I took one of my cigarillos, unique in the fact that I was the only one who smoked them in the area, and placed it softly beside his head. With that, I turned and soundlessly glided away into the darkness.

I occasionally ran into him afterwards, he still hated me and still meant me harm. However, even when I was in situations where I was completely disadvantaged, things would turn around and I would remain unharmed. I like to think that this was due to my observance of what I knew to be right and wrong. A small boon being granted toward my safety for not giving in, for thinking beyond myself even when it offered only hardship and possible harm to do so. The choices we make every day affect the rest of our lives. I'm happy to say that even at my worst, I made a few good ones.

Pleasure Doing Business

Having now spent a long stint at County, I became acutely aware of the monsters residing in the cells on either side of me. More disturbingly, I became acutely aware of the monster that was brewing within myself. Hope was fleeting. I desperately wanted to change, but I knew the odds. Being released into the same circumstances that got me there in the first place would only lead to more of the same.

I needed help. There was a behavioral modification and drug/alcohol program located in Brisbane that I had heard about in passing. Knowing that it was my only chance to make a change, I contacted them and conducted an interview. Once approved, I sent a copy of my acceptance letter to an inmate advocate that helped me with my placement details. The result was a sentence modification that actually extended beyond my original release date, nonetheless, I was sent there immediately. I found it to be a good trade off considering that I had nowhere to go and no way to get to the facility upon my release.

The program in Brisbane was pretty much everything that I expected. Hardcore. It was very structured and aggressively attacked my old ways of thinking. Our hair was all cut to a uniform #2 length and all of our facial hair was eliminated. We were required to shave daily to keep it such. Everything was strictly regimented and we were scrutinized constantly. Any negativity or resistance to the program's principles was dismissed immediately. It was exactly what I needed.

At this point in my life, I desperately needed something to believe in and the principles that they were offering appeared sound. I grasped these said principles and cherished them as my own. We were taught the importance of social responsibility and having a purpose beyond ourselves, about self-reliance and self-respect. Our most important task was to construct a new identity that wasn't tied to our criminal pasts or rooted in old behaviors.

Most of the staff members were ex-cons who knew the real deal. There wasn't anything that they hadn't seen before. They stressed the importance of earning our keep in life; accepting any assistance from family, friends or the government was considered a failure. "Anything not earned, is stolen," they would say.

We secured our places onto different crews and spent our days working hard, learning new trades and re-establishing a solid work ethic. Construction, landscaping and moving companies, a high-end lifestyle retail and design outlet, a cold storage and a package-stuffer assembly line rounded out the diverse list of crews that they had. Not surprisingly, very lucrative contracts were awarded to the program. Just as there was no shortage of work, there was no shortage of nameless convicts to do the work for free. Although this bothered me to some degree, I was much happier here than at County so I didn't complain.

The program basically ran itself. There were three paid employees and the rest of the tasks were done by the hundreds of prisoners that cycled through. Almost all of the food was donated by food banks and charities. There was literally no overhead. We were provided philosophical literature to read, but that was the extent of our schooling. It was a work camp, plain and simple. These things started to gnaw at me, but I tried to stay focused on the positives. I was clean, safe, healthy, well fed, exercising and learning how to think about things in a different manner.

It finally became too much to ignore. After all of their daily rhetoric about not accepting anything that wasn't earned, after all of their derision for section eight and food stamps, after all of this, they required us to apply for EBT and sign it over to them. Of course feeding a hundred inmates wasn't free, but this was in direct contradiction to the very principles that they taught! From that moment on, I saw more and more inconsistencies within both their rhetoric and their application of it.

Although I was extremely rattled by these discoveries, I tried to keep my irritation and frustration to myself. I worked hard, followed the rules and progressed as required. I advanced to the position of weight-training instructor and was allowed to participate in MMA classes where my good attitude and training experience was an attribute to the class. I exceeded every expectation in my work assignments. We had community meetings every Sunday and Wednesday nights. It was at these meetings that problems, concerns, grievances and/or disciplinary measures were aired.

Unfortunately, it was at one of these meetings that my stay was terminated. A senior resident, that I had roomed with for a bit, side busted on a conversation of mine, misread it, and brought it to the groups' attention. I cursed him coarsely and publicly for his idiocy, explaining that he was nothing on the streets and that he was nothing in there. The group facilitator, looking as if I had slapped him, regained his composure and ordered me to leave the facility. They gave me a ride to the BART station and drove away. And there it was... just like that. One slip of my mouth and I was back on the streets.

Deposited in Daly City, I was completely alone. I hadn't a cent in my pocket and knew not one soul. With only the clothes on my back, I foraged some half-smoked cigarette butts from the train station and started walking down Mission Street. I had no idea where I was going but I knew from the map at the bus stop that Mission Street led into the city. I walked all night, feeling hopeless and lost.

Finally, when I was too cold and too tired to walk any further, I took some cardboard from a dumpster, wrapped myself up and curled into a ball on the sidewalk. With the hope that my exhalation would help warm me, I buried my face inside my shirt. Choking back the lump in my throat, I tried to get some rest. I must have fallen asleep, for I awoke with a start to the sound of voices hurriedly passing by. It was raining hard by this time and I tucked closer and closer to the storefront, praying that I wouldn't be noticed by a shopkeeper.

With a stroke of luck, while searching for cigarette butts at the train station the day before, I had found a diamond that had fallen from its mounting. Now, desperate for some hot food, I took it to three different jewelry stores whose signs loudly proclaimed "We Buy

Jewelry". Each one, to my dismay, said that my beautiful stone was merely cubic zirconium and wouldn't give me so much as one dollar for it.

I was crushed. My newfound strength and control began to slip away. It pained me, beyond any hopelessness that I'd ever known, to consider the prospect of looking at the city and its residents with the eyes of a criminal once again. I was becoming desperate and running out of hope. I didn't know what to do. I could see myself slipping into the old patterns that I desperately wanted to forsake.

Angered with myself, I pressed on, refusing to submit to my reckless impulses. I eventually found a County Job Service Agency and stepped inside hoping to find some day labor. After waiting in line for hours, I reached the counter only to be told that my situation required that I talk to a case manager. I took my place in the new line and waited for another hour or so before I was finally able to speak with someone. I outlined what had happened to me to the case worker on duty. She was very helpful, and although unable to get me work, she gave me a list of community resources that I could check out. She also took the time to email my PO in Fresno, outlining my predicament.

To make a long story short, I walked from one end of the city to the other, repeatedly, trying any organization or agency that could potentially help me along the way. To no avail. One afternoon, on Market Street, I was approached by a gentleman that said he had some work for me. He could tell that I was fresh out of prison and pointed out a guy sitting at the bus stop. Although I was disappointed about the nature of the work, I was excited to actually earn some cash.

He waited around the corner while I strode directly up to the guy and started punching him in the face. After a quick six or seven blows, I ran off. The object was not to incapacitate him, but to let him know that this could happen at anytime, anywhere. I met the gentleman where I had left him and put my hand out for payment. He slapped a small package into my hand and said, "Pleasure doing business," before quickly disappearing into the crowd.

My hands shook with rage as I unwrapped it. I wanted to smash and destroy the bag and anyone who came near me. It wasn't money for a bus ticket home. It wasn't money for food. It wasn't money for something to quench my thirst. It was a package of meth. I wanted to cry when I saw it. I had been clean for eleven months. **ELEVEN MONTHS!** I was starting to feel like a real person again. Now this. It hurt so bad knowing that I was going to use it.

Throughout my life I have always turned to drugs. I used when I was happy, to celebrate. I used when I was sad, to escape. There was clearly a void within me and I made it my mission to fill this vacancy with whatever sinful excess I could find. A lifetime of drug abuse culminated in me being physically, mentally and emotionally addicted to a hopeless level. At the peak of my addiction, I was consuming at least an eight ball of meth a day. Until it stopped working. Eventually, the only thing that was left of my life, the only thing that was left of me, brought me no solace. Yet, I was bound to it; it had consumed my soul.

I recently began to explore the deep seated causes of my addiction. It seemed that my discoveries just led to more questions. Why am I never good enough? Why do I fear the things I fear? Why do I feel like, even now, that I am just learning to do the things that everybody else already knows? Well, maybe it's because I always ran when things got tough. Maybe it's because I was always high instead of learning or growing. Maybe it's because instead of addressing and strengthening my weaknesses, I would mask them in a drug-induced euphoria. Feeling fast and strong and powerful was as easy as taking a hit. For a while. Eventually, that's all that was left, the next hit. Then crushing despair. *What now*? I would ask myself. And I had not an answer.

Standing there on the street that day, holding the package of meth, was the loneliest that I have ever felt. No one knew where I was or how to get ahold of me. I had lost all of my contacts so even if I wanted to reach out to someone, I couldn't. There was no safety net, no advantage and no privileges, nobody that could or would help me. It was all up to me. A part of me rose to the challenge, bristling, ready to fight tooth and nail for every bit of my existence. Yet another part of me just wanted to break down and cry, to give up. I was scared and alone and had no idea what to do. So I got high.

I wandered around the Tenderloin and Mission Districts for about a week, eating out of dumpsters, smoking butts off the street and trying to get the lay of the land. Numbness began to set in. I desperately wanted to do things right, but I was exhausting every avenue and coming up empty. Extremely stressed, and ridiculously paranoid from the meth, I could feel my tenuous grip on my sanity slipping. I was in a bad, bad place and I knew that horrible things were to come if things didn't change quickly.

In a desperate gamble, I trekked the long haul to Fort Miley, the VA's stronghold in the city. The work program in Brisbane afforded me one critical item, an ID card. Knowing how important this item was, I kept it on my person and guarded it as if my life depended on it. Ironically, my life actually did depend on it. With this card I was able to receive services at the VA hospital, services that had eluded me in the past without an ID card. They hydrated me with IV fluids, took a battery of tests and kept me in isolation overnight until the headshrinkers could evaluate me the next morning.

After talking to the doctors, explaining my situation and expressing my need for help, I received some solid advice. They informed me that there were many programs available to me and that I would receive VA assistance for pretty much everything that I qualified for. They encouraged me to attend a detox center and referred me to one. I happily complied.

As I walked into the detox center, I felt as if a weight had been lifted off me. I was safe. Somebody cared about what happened to me. There were toilets and showers. A clean bed. Hot meals and coffee. Rolling tobacco was provided at the front desk. The staff was courteous and helpful and genuinely cared about my well-being. I took none of these things for granted. I was so thankful for this care. Most importantly, I was thankful to once again have hope. I needed to do things the right way, and finally, I felt as if I had a fighting chance.

I contacted my PO from the detox center and was told that for every day that I was in San Francisco, I was one more day non-compliant in Fresno. I explained to him that I was struggling to find a way back to Fresno and that I was trying to do the right thing. Let's just say that he wasn't very sympathetic. He responded by saying, "You should have thought of that before you got ejected from the program." It was crushing news. I now had to turn my back on any help offered to me by the VA so that I could clear things up in Fresno.

All told, I was in the detox center for 21 days. After the first 72 hours I was able to start moving about. I used that time to seek out every agency that could possibly help me. Finally, a Veterans Help Agency gave me just enough for a greyhound ticket back to Fresno. I felt pretty optimistic that once I cleared things up with my PO, that the VA would help me get my life back on track. The head lady at the Detox Center wrote me a shining letter detailing my progress and intentions. With that, I said goodbye and embarked at the prescribed time.

I Am Matthew

I arrived back in Fresno late on a Friday afternoon. Nobody knew that I was coming for I had been absent just shy of a year. Having nowhere else to go, I followed the railroad tracks down to my old campsite, unsure of what I would find. Nashelle was still there. She had a new man, but he was in jail. Almost all of my stuff was gone, but she outfitted me with a few articles of clothing. We smoked cigarettes, ate dinner and talked extensively into the night. I told her about my hopes that the VA would help me to get a job and an apartment. I shared with her my plans for change and a better life.

Of course, as the first rays of the sun crept over the horizon, we were once again in each other's arms. Later that day, a few of her acquaintances stopped by for a smoke. I didn't indulge. Not only did I have to see my parole officer the following Monday, but I was clean. Weighing a healthy 240 pounds, as opposed to the 180 pounds that I weighed when I left, I was filled with positive intentions and hope.

Nashelle didn't seem overly supportive of my new attitude, but she loved me, so I received wonderful care the entire weekend. On Monday, she gave me $1.50 for the bus so that I could make it to my appointment with my parole officer. I unknowingly got off at the wrong department so I spent much of the afternoon walking the six miles to the correct one. It was just shy of closing time when I finally arrived. I was immediately arrested. Back to County. Back to the cesspool of negativity. Back to the same criminal culture that I had fought so hard to leave behind.

I just couldn't win. It seemed that every time I tried to do the right thing, something else would knock me back down. During this particular stint, I was there for a little over two months. Although it was short in duration, it was one of my harder sentences to serve because I felt so frustrated and despondent. Upon my release, I immediately went to visit my parole officer. Neither a urinalysis nor check-in was required for another six weeks, so I set out to find work. I moved back to camp and started working for the same tree trimmer that I had been erratically employed with before.

Although I was earning money, it wasn't a good situation. Everyone around me used, most were gang members and quite often crimes were committed on the job. Eventually, I began to use again too. Things were quickly slipping right back to where they had been before. Except for one thing. I had changed. I couldn't live like that anymore. In fact, I became disgusted with the entire situation. It finally became clear to me that, with the exception of Nashelle, not a single person actually cared for me. All anyone cared about was exploiting me for their benefit.

With my first pay in hand, I left everything. The camp. The job. The people. The life. I slept in a dumpster enclosure for the first two nights. I had no idea what to do or where to go, I just knew that I had to do something drastic in order to take responsibility for my life.

In the past I had always worried so much about my companion that I never contemplated leaving, of making a change. At that moment, I made an important connection; I realized that my guilt for leaving my daughters was being manifested by over compensating in my loyalty and protection towards Nashelle. This wasn't about her anymore. This was about me. This was about not making any more excuses.

It was then, while walking through the Fulton open-air Mall, when I finally reached for the pay phone. It was a call that would change my life. Unbeknownst to me, a miraculous chain of events in various parts of the country had already been set into motion. For seven years I had been out of contact, seemingly wiped from the face of the earth to those who loved me. My trail had run cold when I dropped out of society and the last traces of my whereabouts were now years back. Just as I had no way to contact them, they had no way to contact me.

There was little hope for me to be found. My loved ones, hoped against hope, and continued the hunt all the while. They refused to give up on me until news of my life, or death, was obtained. By some miracle, during the brief two month window of time that I had spent at County, I was finally located. Contact information was exchanged, and I ended up with a phone number to call. For the first time in years, when I was at my very lowest and had nowhere else to turn, I finally had someone to reach out to for help. And that is what I did. Within moments of calling, my kin banded together and mobilized, heading to Fresno to find me. For no other reason than they loved me, they came for me.

That was it. It sounds so simple, but yet, it took years to accomplish. With my family at least a day away, I knew that I had to find somewhere safe to stay until they arrived. As soon as I hung up, I walked to the Rescue Mission. Here, men like myself could receive a meal and a bunk in exchange for doing chores and attending a church service. Although I felt hopeful and excited to reunite with my family and to begin my new life, my decision to leave was definitely still gnawing at me. Leaving Nashelle permanently at the mercy of the coarse and filthy streets was almost too much to bear.

I had an insistent, almost frantic, need to tell her what I was going to do. A need for her approval, or endorsement. Or maybe even her anger or hatred. Something, anything, to make this decision easier. Later that day I walked to the store a couple of blocks away from the Rescue Mission to get some cigarettes and a soda. As usual, it was excruciatingly hot out. In an incredible bit of circumstance, I saw one of our old camp-mates at the store buying ice. I asked him to tell Nashelle where I was, that I was ok, and that I was done with this life. I told him that I really needed to see her one last time, that she was important to me.

Time crawled by as I sat on a filthy curb at the corner of two neglected stretches of broken pavement. The sun pressed on and on, higher into the sky, until not even the crumbling warehouses and decrepit service stations offered me refuge from its searing touch. With my shade now completely gone and my soda nothing but a distant memory, I sat alone in misery. By now, my turmoil had reached an indescribable peak. Perhaps it was a self-imposed penance for what was to come, for what I had to do and what I had to say to someone whom I loved.

Just as I knew she would, along the railroad tracks, she came. In a frantic whirlwind of motion, she furiously pedaled her bicycle towards me. I could see her panic evident in her haste to reach me. My heart leapt simultaneously with joy to see her and incredible pain knowing what was to come. Even across the sun-blistered expanse, I could see the tears glistening on her beautiful face. This woman. She had followed me to my worst and beyond. Alone before me, in that desolate wasteland, the dust washed from her face in two tiny trails of tears. "Why? Why poppa? Please don't leave me poppa." The memory of this heart-wrenching farewell will haunt me for the rest of my life.

I told her that she could call my mother's house, that I would do anything that I could to help her. I would. I owed her that. I also told her that my journey was one that I had to undertake alone. She shared her cold beverage with me and I gave her some cigarettes. Then I turned and walked away. Away from the danger. Away from the violence. Away from the deceit. Away from the savagery. Away from the pain. Away from the emptiness. Away from the failure. Away from her. I walked away and left her there, sobbing.

Two days later, I was 1,800 miles away starting a new life. On my own. Learning to stand again. I hope that she did the same. I saw online that our camp had been bulldozed to make way for the new high speed rail line. I can only hope... I can only hope that she's standing too. God bless her and keep her safe.

Just as I'll never forget these experiences, I'll never forget the people. I met some of the most amazing and incredibly talented artists, musicians, craftsmen and poets. I also met some of the most malicious and abominable murderers, rapists and criminally insane menaces. And then there were the girls. So many damaged girls. Ghosts of whatever trauma had damaged them, now driving an endless cycle of repetition and perpetuation of these same abuses. It was staggering to me, this world.

I think worse than the bleak despair that I saw in people's eyes, was when I saw the dull glint of resignation. The bottom line is, when you are living like an animal, you start to think like one. Not just in a good way, such as sharpened survival instincts, but with regards to cognitive perception. It falls to the wayside in a world like this. You lose track of things like principles and philosophy, everything beyond yourself faded and lost as you surrender to sustaining your basic needs. No sense of purpose. No goals or aspirations beyond tomorrow. No cares for anyone or anything. No dreams.

It truly is the death of humanity, the loss of these subtle aspects of life. There are many who would never bounce back if given the opportunity, too lost for too long. But many would. I have. Against the craftiest of foe, against the cruelty of the words and thoughts that sometimes ring in my head, against all odds, I have come to live again.

With everything stripped away, I learned many things. I learned that I didn't really know anything about life. I also learned that I didn't really know anything about myself. My illusions and thoughts of who I was and how things were, became further stained with each passing day and eventually were shattered. What I have learned, is that both success and failure, happiness and sadness, are sculpted by perspective. Everything is. Every choice that I make is affected by my perspective. The experiences that I have shared with you in this book have been extremely painful for me to endure. However, I never could have reached the levels of understanding and shifts of perspective that I currently hold, had I not gone through them. I've evolved. I understand now that *this* moment is the most important moment, not because the past or future doesn't matter, but because *this* moment is the only one that I can control. I can't control anyone or anything around me. Just me. This is a very powerful discovery and it wasn't until I was stripped of absolutely everything, that I was able to unearth it. *I* choose who I am this minute and the next. No one else.

In the end, it was the people who love me and divine intervention that brought me out. It also took me having some good left inside, something that was worth saving. It took me clinging to the tiny murmur within me that said that I deserved more. That I was worth something. That life could still be beautiful, even for me. Even after all that I had done wrong, and all that I had failed at. These are battles that I still fight. Only time, hard work and God's grace will help me to see the Matthew that is seen by the people who love me. I'm going to keep trying. Every minute. Every day. Striving to be the man that I want to be. I owe it to myself. I owe it to those who love me.

I am thankful.

I am blessed.

I am Matthew.

About the Author

Matthew Davidson was born on September 15, 1972 in Anchorage, Alaska. A few years later, he moved to Southeast Alaska where he spent the majority of his childhood. After graduating from Haines High School in 1990, he embarked for basic training in Ft. Knox, Kentucky. Following completion, he served with the Blackhorse Regiment in Germany, as well as in Kuwait during Desert Shield and Desert Storm.

Once his enlistment term was completed, Matthew returned to Southeast Alaska where he initially worked in the commercial fishing and crabbing industry. He eventually settled into the construction trade before his incarceration in 1995. Upon his release in 1998, he resided briefly in Seattle before returning once again to Southeast Alaska. Here, Matthew got married, began raising his two daughters and continued to advance in his chosen craft of construction.

In 2006, fresh on the heels of a divorce, Matthew made his new home in Fresno, California, where he continued to work in the construction trade. In 2010, Matthew became homeless. Three grueling years later, in July of 2013, his family came for him. He moved to the Midwest where he slowly began to piece his life back together. During this time, Matthew found love and, in the fall of 2014, they exchanged vows. He continues to reside in the Midwest with his new bride.

Made in the USA
Coppell, TX
08 April 2022

76185127R00083